D1559115

INFLUENCING THROUGH ARGUMENT
Updated Edition

international debate education association

New York - Amsterdam - Brussels

INFLUENCING THROUGH ARGUMENT
Updated Edition

Robert B. Huber
with
Alfred C. Snider

Published by
International Debate Education Association
400 West 59th Street
New York, NY 10019

Library of Congress Cataloging-in-Publication Data

Huber, Robert B.
 Influencing through argument / Robert B. Huber with Alfred C.
Snider.-- Updated ed.
    p. cm.
 ISBN 1-932716-07-6
        978-1-932716-07-8 (alk. paper)
 1. Persuasion (Rhetoric) 2. Reasoning. I. Snider, Alfred. II. Title.

PN4121.H78 2005
808--dc22
                    2005010906

Printed in the USA

 IDEBATE Press Books

Contents

Chapter 8
Influencing Through Causal Reasoning

Chapter 9
Influencing Through Reasoning from Analogy

Notes About the Updated Edition

I have been very pleased at how popular the web version of this textbook has been. Students and teachers have thanked me for making it available at no cost. Surprisingly, people began to ask if there was a way we could produce a print copy that they could purchase. I did this through the Debate Publication program at the University of Vermont [http://debate.uvm.edu/ee.html] and the roughly bound laser print copies were increasingly popular.

The International Debate Education Association (IDEA) indicated their interest in publishing a new edition of the book. Their logic was that many people want a solid hard copy to use and that this was a good resource for students and teachers of argumentation and debate. I accepted their offer to make some changes and publish a 2006 print edition.

I have made a number of changes in this edition, though the basic text remains. I have updated the examples used to better reach a twenty-first century international audience. I have further adjusted the pronouns used in the text to reflect modern use. I have also added a few small sections to highlight material not in the original text.

Once again, every good part of this text is because of the fine work of Robert Huber, and every bad part of this text is my responsibility.

I would like to thank Noel Selegzi of IDEA and Martin Greenwald of the Open Society Institute for their support of this project.

The basic ideas of argumentation and reasoning remain secure through the passage of time. Every citizen needs these skills in order to help contribute to a better future.

Think for yourself!

Alfred C. Snider
Edwin W. Lawrence Professor of Forensics, University of Vermont
August 2005

ROBERT HUBER, 1909-1996
A Life of Influence and Integrity

No one is really in a good position to judge anyone's life, and I certainly can't, but I want to share with you a few of my thoughts.

Robert Huber changed many thousands of lives for the better. He taught people how to speak and also how to speak up. He told me that he believed he had instructed more students in basic public speaking over 51 years than any human ever. He coached debate at the University of Vermont (UVM) from 1946 until 1983, influencing thousands of students who went on to make a real difference for the better in the world.

Robert Huber built institutions to carry on his work. He was extremely important in the Speech Communication Association, the Eastern Communication Association, Delta Sigma Rho-Tau Kappa Alpha, and other groups. He arranged to have the UVM debate team secured with an endowment and then helped create an endowed professorship for the team's debate coach. He organized summer debate institutes at UVM for decades, paving the way for the current World Debate Institute held at UVM each summer. The annual UVM debate tournament has, for many years, been named after Robert Huber. We call our offices at 475 Main Street "Huber House."

Robert Huber was a debate innovator with an impressive record of competitive success. His teams were well prepared and gave excellent presentations. Although he was modest, he seems to have been the inventor of the modern "plan" wherein his teams would not support the entire resolution, but would support the resolution through their specific proposal.

Robert "Doc" Huber was personally very helpful to me. When I arrived at UVM to assume the Lawrence professorship, his advice was keen, useful, and accurate. I think about how lucky I am today to be doing what I am doing where I am doing it, and I know that without Doc's work and effort none of this would be here for my students and myself.

Robert Huber promoted discussion and debate as the model for citizenship. When an alumnus donated a car, he and the debaters began barnstorming Vermont—bringing debates and discussions to every small town they could, and it went on for years and years. Today we have a weekly television program that tries to capture the same spirit.

The ultimate product of our profession as debate coaches is a body of concerned, critically thinking, intelligent, and communicative citizens who can take the tragedy of today and turn it into the victories of tomorrow by working hard, by thinking deeply, and by speaking out. In the government, in the professions, in business, and all over the world, his outstanding students are an important legacy.

Robert Huber certainly stands out as a giant in his profession.

Alfred C. Snider
Edwin W. Lawrence Professor of Forensics, University of Vermont
June 1996

INFLUENCING THROUGH ARGUMENT
Updated Edition

Chapter 1
Why Use Argument to Influence Others?

ARGUMENT WIDELY USED

The president of the corporation stands and says: "Will the meeting please come to order? I have called this meeting of the executive council to consider the new proposal of Ms. Jones, our personnel manager, to improve our method of securing employees." The meeting continues with Ms. Jones presenting her proposal. If Ms. Jones does well, she presents carefully constructed arguments to prove why a new method is needed and shows how her proposal will improve recruitment. Organizations throughout the world daily consider many such proposals, with committees hearing arguments for adoption or rejection and making decisions based on what they hear.

The chairperson speaks: "Our committee, as you know, has been appointed by the president of the university to consider the best methods for raising endowments. Ms. James has a method that she wishes to suggest for our consideration." Ms. James then proceeds to explain her plan and present arguments in its favor. She reveals how other colleges have had great success with similar plans. This is typical of the meetings of committees of all kinds of institutions and organizations in which argument plays a dominant role.

The gavel raps and the courtroom quiets. The judge announces: "The prosecuting attorney will now sum up the case for the prosecution." This public official then proceeds to use the evidence presented through the days of examining witnesses to draw conclusions for the jury to evaluate in determining the guilt or innocence of the accused. This process is one of presenting arguments.

Ms. Brown comes to the reception area and greats Mr. Smith. The young woman speaks: "I am Ms. Brown from the Mutual Life Insurance Company.

You made an appointment with me to go over your insurance program. Please come into my office." Together Mr. Smith and Ms. Brown analyze his insurance policies. If Ms. Brown is successful in presenting arguments for more insurance, she will make a sale. Here we see an example of the use of argument in the daily work of salespeople regardless of what they sell—insurance, new refrigerators, automobiles, brands of food, or new homes.

Throughout our daily lives, we use argument to decide what we will buy, what college we shall attend, or where we will go on vacation. Gathering material for the presentation of arguments is a major task for members of parliaments and legislatures, of city councils, of town meetings, and of local and state commissions. The presentation of arguments is the chief aim of public forums, discussions, and debates. Therefore, a democracy with the goal of developing each individual to his or her highest leadership potential should encourage and support the development of the highest skill in the art of argumentation. Those who want to be leaders must develop this skill if they are to influence others.

THE PSYCHOLOGICAL NEED FOR GOOD ARGUMENT

Self-esteem demands that you and I have the best set of reasons possible for any action we take. We need the security of belief that our behavior is justifiable to ourselves. We must be able to defend our behavior to our parents, wives, husbands, sweethearts, and friends. In fact, we feel silly when we cannot. For example, President George W. Bush justified his invasion of Iraq by arguing that it has weapons of mass destruction it could use against the United States and that it was a haven for terrorists. Within all of us is a psychological need for a good set of arguments to defend or justify any action we take.

ARGUMENT DEFINED

Argument, then, may be defined as that process in communication in which logic is used to influence others. This sometimes takes the form of reinforcing old attitudes. More often, however, argument is used to attempt to change attitudes or to establish new ones. Argument is used to influence those around us either through the spoken or written word. We should recognize that much that is called argument is not; it is merely the expression of "my opinion" over and against "your opinion." This is often the form of late night discussions and social conversations. The real process of argument is the process of demonstrating conclusions from facts or premises that have been established as truths. Remember that the goal of argument is influencing attitudes and is not exhibitionism; it is to influence conduct and not just to engage in a dispute.

ARGUMENT IS ONLY ONE PHASE OF PERSUASION

Persuasion may be defined as "the process of influencing the conduct or attitudes of others." Argument may be described as "the logical mode of persuasion." The Greek rhetoricians gave this the name of *logos*. A second phase of persuasion is an appeal to the emotions. This is sometimes called "the psychological mode of persuasion." The Greek rhetoricians gave this the name of *pathos*. Still a third phase of persuasion is that residing in the speaker or author. The prestige of the individual who says something affects the statement's power to persuade. The name given by the Greeks to this was *ethos*. The word *ethical* in this context differs somewhat from the more common meaning of good moral behavior. The two meanings are not totally unrelated, however, as through the ages many have believed that the ethical appeal of a speaker is weak unless she is a woman of good moral character. A fourth phase of persuasion pertains to **style.** Skillful use of language—words, phrases, and sentences, along with special rhetorical devices, such as figures of speech, allusions, and groupings of three—adds to the forcefulness of a speaker's or writer's argument.

The main portion of this book will be devoted almost entirely to the logical mode of persuasion. The last chapter will give a brief discussion of the other phases as they pertain to argumentative speech.

THE PROCESSES OF ARGUMENT AND THE PROCESSES OF REASONING

Reasoning is the process of drawing conclusions from facts or premises. In reasoning from analogy and in inductive reasoning, we start with factual examples and from them we draw conclusions. Some parts of causal reasoning may be reasoning from facts. On the other hand, when we engage in deductive reasoning and some phases of causal reasoning, we draw conclusions from premises, or truths that have come to be believed. Often these truths have been established earlier by facts. Argument differs from the reasoning process only in that the former is used in a communicative process and that it is chiefly a demonstration to others of the reasoning process that the speaker or writer has worked through. Ms. Jones, the personnel manager cited in the example above, would ordinarily go through a variety of reasoning processes to arrive at the new proposal. As she has done that, her presentation of arguments is merely the demonstration of those selected reasoning processes that convinced her that the proposed solution was a good one. In essence, then, the argumentative process is merely demonstrating to others the steps in reasoning by which we arrived at our own conclusions.

ARGUMENT AND EMOTION

Argument cannot be divorced from emotion. The person skilled in influencing others in argument must be aware that the strongest arguments are usually those that are based on the strongest emotions. In addition, the "cost" argument will always carry strong weight—people can be persuaded to follow courses of action that serve their needs and wants.

THE STUDY OF ARGUMENT VERSUS THE STUDY OF LOGIC

The goal of the study of logic is knowledge of thought processes. It might be defined as the science of thought or as a science that investigates the process of thinking. The study of argumentation, on the other hand, is the study of the art of influencing others by reasoned discourse—the aim of which is to get others to believe or to act as the speaker or writer wishes. To achieve this goal, an individual must first study logic as a science and then develop its use in argumentation. Logic is a science that teaches us to know, while argumentation is an art teaching us to do; logic is the science of which argumentation is the corresponding art.

GROWING DEMANDS FOR ARGUMENT

As the world's population becomes better educated and the literacy level rises, the demand for improved argumentative processes increases. As people attain more knowledge, they become better critics and more capable of making better evaluations of conclusions. The average adult in the latter part of the nineteenth century had only achieved about a fifth or sixth grade education. The average adult of today has much more and thus is turning more strongly to argument. The speaker of tomorrow will find even greater demands for clear reasoning, and so we may expect that the demand for better and better arguments will increase.

The Role of Argument

In Advocacy

An advocate is an individual who intentionally tries to influence the attitudes and beliefs of others on a particular topic or topics—for example, advocates of free trade, advocates of socialism, or advocates of free enterprise. *Advocacy* is the term applied to the act of espousing and supporting a cause or idea. The substance with which the advocate deals is transformed into arguments; he pleads his cause by developing arguments that constitute reasons for believing. Ideally, an advocate is an individual who has studied a question thoroughly, formed conclusions about what should be done, and then proceeds to bring others to his cause by force of argument. Advocacy is not objective in nature nor is the advocate an impartial investigator. You, as a student of argument, should take the role of an advocate in your prepared speeches and plead for the belief of the audience on subjects of your choice. At other times, you should take the role of a severe critic evaluating the conclusions of others by testing the soundness of the reasoning from which their conclusions are drawn. By taking these two disparate positions, you will advance more rapidly in your understanding of argument.

In Propaganda

Propaganda is an organized effort to influence the attitudes or conduct of others and might be defined as an organized effort at persuasion. The propagandist makes use of argument, employs emotional appeals, utilizes the influence of persons in prominent positions, and attempts to couch her persuasion in the best possible language. Many people react negatively to the word *propaganda*. Some will even try to define it as something bad. We also propagandize for good causes, however, and can hardly say the causes we support are good while the causes of others are bad. The student of argumentation will learn to use effective arguments to support those causes that she advocates and will learn to evaluate for audiences the fallacies in the propaganda of others.

In Education and Learning

Education is the process of imparting knowledge and developing skills. It should be an impartial, objective process, and is, in many ways, the opposite of advocacy and propaganda. The classroom teacher is not an advocate; she is an individual who helps students uncover knowledge and also supports the development of reasoning powers in her students. The teacher allows the student to draw her own conclusions about the events and affairs of the world. The word *education* is often misused. We hear people say, "We must educate people for democracy," or "We must educate people for a capitalist way of life." Often they mean *propagandize*, not *educate*. Many maintain that argument should be minimized in teaching and that the teacher's only job is to persuade students to study harder or to develop their skills more rapidly. On the other hand, the study of the arguments by which humankind arrived at decisions in the past becomes an important part of the education of all of us. We can observe those who have been misled as well as those who have been pointed in apparently more logical directions. The student of argument, however, will find training in argument valuable because the reasoning process is an essential part of understanding the world. Thus, increased knowledge of argument, which results in increased knowledge of the reasoning process, should reinforce learning.

In Inquiries and Investigations

An inquirer or an investigator is someone who tries to discover the truth about something. He starts out saying, "I don't know what is true about this situation, but I shall try to find out." He may suspect certain things to be true and set up a hypothesis. The inquirer/investigator has an open mind, is impartial and objective, and is quite willing to admit it if the facts do not support his hypothesis. An advocate is the opposite; an advocate may have started out as an inquirer but the facts forced her to arrive at a conclusion that she then began to champion. As in education, the reasoning process is an important tool of the inquirer or investigator; argument has little place in this process. The student of argumentation, however, as she uses the reasoning process, can become a good investigator if she can maintain the greatest possible objectivity during the investigation. Once the investigation is complete and the truth has been discovered, the inquirer might then become an advocate. Many inquirers/investigators go astray when they allow their suppositions to color the interpretations of their findings. Any slight bit of evidence that supports their hypothesis is often inflated or distorted to support their hypothesis.

In Discussion

Discussion may be defined as a cooperative venture in group thinking and is often characterized as being objective and impartial. In most cases advocates are not wanted because they are not sufficiently impartial and objective. The student of argument, however, who has studied the fallacies in the reasoning process and is expert in revealing these fallacies to others, can be of great help. The very process of discussion is one of using the reasoning process—facts are brought into the discussion and from those facts and other premises the group draws its conclusions. As an individual participates in a problem solving discussion and begins to evaluate proposed solutions, debating the various solutions offered will test them one against the other with, in the most desired outcome, the best solution being decided upon. The student of argument, in her study of the reasoning process, can become a superior individual in discussion if she is able to curb any tendencies to be an advocate.

In Debate

Debate is the process of presenting arguments for or against a proposition. Propositions for which people argue are controversial and have one or more individuals presenting the case for the proposition while others present the case against it. Every debater is an advocate; the purpose of each speaker is to gain the belief of the audience for his side. Argument is the core of the debate speech—the superior debater must be superior in the use of argument. The chief means of persuasion in debate is the logical mode.

Debate is an inherent in democracy and is used in many phases of life. Presidential candidates use it in campaigning. Members of Congress, state legislators, and local governing boards debate the laws and ordinances that they are considering enacting. The nations of the world debate programs and resolutions within the United Nations. Educators as well as investigators debate the soundness of conclusions. Those participating in discussion will often use debate when trying to determine "What is the best solution?" In any phase of life, when confronted with problems, people will often find debate a superior method of testing solutions to discover the best. So important is debate within a democracy and in solving daily problems, that progressive high schools and colleges offer strong programs of formal interscholastic debate. Progressive educators know that training in debate is training in argument, that training in argument is training in logic, and that logic is the basis of critical thinking.

In Rhetorical Criticism

Criticism may be defined as the process of evaluating the worth of a thing, particularly when we are considering art, literature, or formal rhetoric. In the twentieth century great advances have been made in the area of rhetorical criticism—the study of great speeches and great speakers. Experts in rhetoric and public address have studied these speeches and perorations and have made critical evaluations of them. Surveys of rhetorical criticism, such as the excellent book by Sonja Foss (2004), *Rhetorical Criticism: Exploration and Practice*, discuss past masters of persuasive rhetoric and give examples. True criticism, which is both impartial and objective, makes great use of the reasoning processes but avoids advocacy. At most, arguments tend to be limited to those necessary to support the critic's conclusions on the worth of the speeches or the eminence of the speaker. The student of argumentation, on the other hand, if he can suppress tendencies toward advocacy, can be a better critic for having studied the reasoning processes of others. In fact, some of the better courses preparing an individual for graduate study are logic and argumentation.

ELEMENTS OF THE STUDY OF ARGUMENT

Before going further, let us pause to get a bird's eye view of what we are about to study. First, we must learn the kinds of subjects that demand argument. Some subjects demand reasoned discourse as their mode of development; with others emotional appeals must be basic or virtually constitute the entire speech. Second, we must learn how to analyze propositions so that we may select and build the best arguments on a subject. The third part is to study the methods by which we can quickly, yet effectively, gather material essential to supporting our arguments. Fourth, we shall look at evidence and the lines of argument by which we can make effective use of it, either in building our speeches or in evaluating those of others. As the substance of argument is inductive, deductive, causal, or analogical reasoning, our fifth task must be to study these kinds of reasoning along with the lines of argument best suited to each. Within a democracy pressure groups or individuals are always advocating the adoption of unwise or inferior courses of action, therefore, we must be prepared to reveal their weaknesses. Sixth, we shall concern ourselves with refutation, the study of revealing fallacies.

Although this volume mainly discusses the logical mode of persuasion, we must remember that logic is not enough. After making sure that our logical structure is sound, we must go further and recognize and use some of the nonlogical means of persuasion to reinforce our arguments. Chapter 11 briefly describes these nonlogical elements.

EXERCISES

1. Define the following concepts:
    a. Argument
    b. Persuasion
    c. Reasoning
    d. Logic
    e. Logos
    f. Pathos
    g. Ethos
    h. Style
    i. Evidence
    j. Propaganda
    k. Education
    l. Inquiry
    m. Discussion
    n. Rhetorical criticism
2. Why should we use argument to influence others?
3. List areas not mentioned by the authors in which argument is widely used today.
4. Where might you expect to use argument during your college career?
5. In what situations do you expect to use argument in your professional life after graduation?
6. Differentiate between *argument* and *persuasion*.
7. What is the difference between reasoning and argument?
8. How does the study of logic in the department of philosophy differ from the study of argument in a speech department?

9. Contrast the role of the advocate and that of a participant in discussion.

10. How does propaganda differ from persuasion?

11. Explain what is meant by, and defend the proposition that, "teachers should seldom be advocates." List some of the exceptions to that statement and defend each.

12. Should certain ethical principles guide those who use argument? If so, what are they? For example, should an advocate plead for something that would be good for her own geographic area but would bring injustice to the state or the nation? Legislators are sometimes confronted with this dilemma.

Chapter 2
With What Kinds of Subjects Is Argument Effective?

Now that we have observed that argument is widely used and is being demanded more and more as people become more educated and have seen what the nature of argument is, we may well ask in what areas is argument most effective? In other words, what is worth arguing about and what isn't worth arguing about?

PROPOSITIONS AS SUBJECTS FOR ARGUMENT

A proposition is an assertion that an advocate intends to prove to an audience in the form of a complete sentence. Furthermore, it is a sentence about which individuals disagree. The speaker may consider such topics as school spirit, AIDS prevention, or automobile accidents. Although these phrases might make excellent titles for speeches or compositions, as subjects on which to present arguments they are valueless. On the other hand, if we phrase propositions about certain aspects of each of the foregoing subjects over which opinions might differ, we will have proper subjects for argumentation. For example, the proposition, "College athletes should be given scholarships," is a good one about which to present arguments either pro or con. This is particularly true when many members of your audience are opposed to such a policy. If the audience of students, alumni, and faculty to whom you are speaking is in complete agreement with you that college athletes should be given scholarships, you need not take the time to develop well-supported arguments. Your object in this case would be to get group action toward raising money for those scholarships. At best, you would start the speech for action by briefly summarizing the arguments constituting the basis of their belief and then proceed to stir the audience into action.

Subjects for argument must be in the form of propositions that are phrased in such a way that disagreement exists.

Purpose of Speakers Using Argument

In building any speech, we must clearly state our specific purpose. In a speech using argument, the general purpose is to gain belief. The specific purpose is to gain belief on the proposition presented. In the example above, the specific purpose would probably be worded as follows: "To gain the belief of the audience that athletic scholarships should be awarded at university X." So, carefully craft the proposition for your whole speech and then place the words "to gain belief of the audience" in front of it. This is one of the cornerstones of a superior speech. The specific purpose becomes the guide that dictates what you should include and what you should not. A carefully expressed specific purpose will help you avoid irrelevancies and keep you from wandering from the subject. Place your well-worded specific purpose at the top of the final outline of the speech to help you keep your focus.

Types of Propositions

Your study of argumentation will be aided by an understanding of the different kinds of propositions. Each kind has its own particular methods for analysis, its own particular structure of arguments required for its development, its own particular methods of approach in refutation. At this point in your study of argument you would be wise to develop the skill of identifying the nature of proposition you are engaging.

Fact

A proposition of fact asserts the truth or falsity of some factual matter. In the courtroom, many of the cases are propositions of fact. "John Jones is a murderer"; "Jack Smith is a burglar." A trial is conducted to establish the truth or falsity of that proposition. The prosecuting attorney and the defense attorney argue over whether or not the charge is a statement of fact. We often argue over propositions about exactly what happened in the past or what may happen in the future. For many years any number of individuals in the United States tried to determine the actual cost of building an underground highway system beneath Boston, with much disagreement about the actual figures and years of discussion about the facts.

Another proposition of fact that has concerned us for some time is the degree of human influence on climate. The proposition that many are debating is: "Increased use of fossil fuels is causing global warming." Such propositions of fact are worthy of consideration and argument since there are many gaps between the amount of evidence available and the complete establishment of the truth or falsity of this statement.

Value

A proposition of value asserts the worth of something. In recent years people have debated the propositions: "The idea of freedom has been taken too far in Western societies" and "We may need to sacrifice some of our liberties to guarantee safety from terrorism." For many years Americans have debated the proposition: "The use of the Electoral College in selecting the president is not democratic." Often you will find yourself developing arguments on propositions of value about the worth of some policy, action, or thing.

Policy

Probably the greatest numbers of propositions that you will be building arguments to influence belief are propositions of policy, which propose a course of action or a solution and are easily identified because the word should appear within the proposition. Specific examples of propositions of policy are: "Our corporation should raise the price of its product"; "The executive branch of our government should be reorganized"; "We should hire The High Fliers band for our sorority party"; "We should buy a new automobile."

In summary, we note that the proposition of fact is one in which we are trying to determine whether a particular statement is actually true. In the proposition of value, we are concerned with the worth of the thing we are talking about. In the proposition of policy, we are trying to determine what course of action we should take in the future. In Chapter 3, "Analysis and Definition," we will examine the differences among these propositions so as to discover the arguments necessary to prove them. In Chapter 7, "Influencing Through Deduction," we shall discover the type of reasoning essential to proving various phases of these propositions. It should also be noted that there is a definite interrelationship among the three types of propositions. A proposition of fact may constitute a complete discussion in itself. Often, however, propositions of fact may be subpropositions to those of value or policy. The proposition of policy, however, contains propositions of both fact and value as subpropositions. As we shall soon learn, in a proposition of policy, an advocate argues that a new course of action is of higher value than one that has been followed and that we should therefore adopt it. Subpropositions of fact, on the other hand, are used by an advocate in an attempt to prove the inferiority of an old policy and the superiority of the proposed new policy.

TESTING YOUR PROPOSITION

The same tests that you applied to subjects in your beginning course in public speaking should be applied to propositions; you want to be sure that the proposition you are going to discuss is worthy. Thus, you should apply the following tests.

Am I Interested or Can I Become Interested in the Proposition?

You will be effective as a speaker only on those subjects that concern or interest you. The greater your interest in a topic, the greater the chance you have in achieving success in its discussion. What subjects might interest you? Usually those about which you have greater knowledge. However, do not cast aside a subject because you do not know much about it. Remember—interest grows with knowledge. The college student taking chemistry for the first time may not be very interested in the subject. But as he learns more about it, he may take additional courses and even decide to become a chemist.

Will My Audience Wish to Hear Me Discuss the Topic?

This test is a double-edged one. Audiences wish to hear the discussion of topics that concern them, that pertain to their daily lives, that are related to their basic wants and desires; they also want to hear from speakers who know more about the proposition than they do. So, in addition to discovering if the subject is related to the basic wants and needs of the audience, speakers must make themselves credible to the audience. A college student speaking on "better business methods" would hardly be acceptable to an audience of businesspeople and that audience would most likely reject her conclusions.

Is It Timely?

A timely topic is one of present concern. We can do nothing now about the proposition, "The North should not have followed a policy of Radical Reconstruction in the South following the Civil War." The problems of social and economic equality that confront us today are those that will receive an audience's continuing attention. Make sure your proposition is timely.

Is It Suitable for the Occasion?

Individuals are usually asked to speak for a specific occasion, possibly as frequent as classroom lectures or as rare as the celebration of a community holiday. Always ask what the occasion is and then be sure to pick a proposition that fits the occasion. The proposition, "Our college should grant more scholarships to athletes," may seem related but is hardly the subject to be discussed at a pep rally prior to a football game. The proposition, "The United Nations Security Council should be expanded," is hardly suitable for the occasion of a celebration of the founding of a young people's group in a church. In many cases, presenting a speech to gain belief or to utilize argument shows lack of judgment.

Is It Narrow Enough to Be Covered Within the Time Limits?

Some propositions take much more time to cover adequately than others. The time needed is dependent on how many main issues are involved and have to be proved. The proposition that the "divorce rate is distinctly higher than it was 50 years ago" should take much less time to establish than the proposition that "the states should adopt uniform divorce laws." The former might be developed sufficiently in 2 to 4 minutes, while the latter would require at least 15 minutes and could well be the subject for a discussion of 40 minutes or longer. All propositions of policy tend to take longer than other types because more issues and subissues are involved. On the other hand, to establish propositions of value, which may need as many as six or eight basic arguments, may take too long. Thus, in picking your proposition, be sure it is narrow enough to be covered in the allotted time. Do not risk the failure resulting from insufficient time to develop your argument.

Is It Suitable for Oral Presentation?

In your beginning work in public speaking you learned that certain topics cannot be presented orally in the classroom. A person cannot learn to swim in a classroom, but a speech about swimming techniques is quite worthwhile at a swimming pool. So, to present an effective speech, the audience must be in the area where the subject can be taught. In the same fashion many propositions are not suitable for oral presentation. Some may become more suitable if you use such visual aids as PowerPoint presentations, DVDs, video clips, diagrams, or charts. This is particularly true when the proposition demands considerable use of statistics. If the statistics can be simplified and put on charts so that the audience can see them, your subject may become suitable for oral presentation. Accordingly, one of the important characteristics of your proposition is that it be suitable for oral presentation.

Is It Subject to Disagreement?

The most frequent purpose of using argument is to change attitudes or beliefs. You choose to argue on propositions about which some members of your audience will disagree; your purpose is to change their belief. If everyone in the audience agrees with you, then the usual reason for speaking is to arouse them emotionally, and possibly to action, about the issue. Most people agree to the proposition that we should give to various well-known charities. Thus, you wouldn't present arguments in the drive to raise money for such charities; rather you would attempt to engage the emotions of the audience. Likewise, a debater would not have to build arguments on the proposition: "Republicans are best to govern America" if the audience was composed only of Republican state chairpersons.

Although a speaker need not use a logical mode of persuasion for an audience that already believes in the proposition that he is advancing, sometimes a speaker will use elements of the logical mode of persuasion in speeches in which he is trying to arouse the audience emotionally. For example, everyone knows that we should drive more carefully. We don't have to present arguments for it. In a speech to stimulate an audience to drive more carefully, however, the speaker may use what appears to be a logical approach. Her main headings may seem to be reasons for believing. The support material may consist of statements of authorities, statistics, and factual examples. In this case, although the speaker may seem to be using the logical mode of persuasion on a proposition, her actual purpose is to get the audience emotionally committed to doing what they already know they ought to do. Thus, although exceptions may appear to exist, only those propositions that are subject to disagreement are worthy of development with argument.

Is It Clear Rather than Ambiguous?

Any term with two or more meanings is ambiguous. Many words or terms do have two or more meanings and, hence, avoiding ambiguity is often difficult. Strive to word your proposition as clearly as possible.

The proposition that "the United States should adopt socialized medicine" uses the extremely ambiguous term *socialized*, which has been defined in many different ways. This proposition could be reworded to state that "the federal government should guarantee medical care for all citizens." This is a better wording; however, the term *medical care* is still ambiguous and would cause difficulty. The speaker might get out of difficulty by explaining what "medical care" includes (e.g., primary, preventive, and rehabilitative care but not long-term custodial care). In choosing and wording your proposition, be as clear as possible and avoid ambiguous terms.

Is It Capable of Being Supported with Evidence?

Theoretical arguments are interesting but the speaker has little chance to gain the belief of an audience unless facts are presented that support the conclusion. Reasoning is a process of drawing conclusions from facts, and the proposition that has too few or no facts to support it will hardly be worth discussing. To present arguments to an audience in your hometown that a sewage disposal plant should be constructed is valuable for discussion only if facts are available to prove it. What kind of facts would support that argument? Water pollution statistics, an outline of the problems of disposal would be a start. In addition, you would need facts about the cost of a sewage disposal plant for your hometown, and so on. Without these facts, your discussion would be useless.

An example of another kind of subject often discussed is: "Was George Washington or Abraham Lincoln the greater president?" This is a question that cannot be answered—no direct evidence is available to establish such a proposition. Was one more capable of performing a particular kind of task than the other? With no direct evidence, we cannot answer the question. A characteristic of a good proposition is that it is capable of being supported with evidence. Thus, these kinds of propositions are not good ones for fruitful debate.

Is It Significant Enough to Be Worthy of Discussion?

What value is there in the ancient argument over how many angels can stand on the head of a pin? Little or none. Likewise, most of the arguments over what section of the country is best as a place to live contain little of real value. Most arguments of this nature merely end up as "my opinion against yours." Don't waste the time of your audience, use your time as speaker to address the problems in the world that need solving, causes that need sponsoring, the many injustices that need correcting.

Is There a Basis for Comparison?

Most propositions, particularly those of value and policy, have comparison as the basis for development. In propositions of value we are asserting the worth of some idea or thing. The proposition: "Wal-Mart stores are beneficial to a community," can be proved only in terms of comparison with the smaller and independent store. Propositions of policy are decided by audiences on the basis of comparing the worth of the old system to the value of the new. Only when the new is shown to be superior to the old will they adopt it. As comparison is the basis of many propositions, it is essential that a sound basis for such comparison exist. The proposition above, "Lincoln was a greater president than Washington" is poor because little exists to make a comparison. They performed different tasks, lived in different ages, and were confronted by vastly different problems. The proposition, therefore, is virtually unprovable and the likelihood of drawing sound conclusions is nil.

Does the Proposition Involve a Single Subject?

Many propositions can be so worded as to involve several plans of action. In the 1990s, the Republican members of the U.S. Congress argued for a "Contract with America." That proposition had many different subjects and would, accordingly, be a poor proposition to advance in a single discussion because of its many parts. An evening would barely suffice to cover even one facet. A speaker addressing the "Contract" would make a stronger presentation if he chose just one of those subjects and advanced arguments for or against it. To attempt to argue such a multiplicity of subjects in one speech would lead to such superficial treatment as to be valueless.

Still another proposition of recent times has been: "A social safety net should be adopted." This, likewise, is a poor proposition because so many programs are involved. The social safety net probably includes, in the minds of most speakers, government health insurance, social security retirement benefits, a program of unemployment insurance, mental health services, and others. Again, the multiplicity of subjects involved would make any discussion of this proposition poor because each could only be treated superficially.

WORDING THE PROPOSITION

Not only should we know the characteristics of a good proposition, we should also know how to word the topic we choose for general and special occasions.

General Occasions

Sometimes the proposition is formally worded for general occasions, more often it is not. If you have been called on to speak and you have a proposition that you want to advance, you would be wise to consider whether or not you should introduce it early in the speech. For example, if you were to tell the audience in your introduction that you were going to try to convince them that "you should refrain from creating too much credit card debt," their reaction might be, "Oh yeah, just try living without credit cards." If you think that the announcement of your overall proposition early in your speech would get a "no" response, you would be wise to hold your announcement for later. You might use a question form to avoid a "no" response or you might merely announce your subject as a phrase, for example, "I'm going to talk to you tonight on the subject of living beyond your means." You, of course, are quite well aware of your proposition and can bring it out in the conclusion of your speech. Speakers giving goodwill speeches seldom announce their proposition even in the conclusion because of the danger of a "no" response. The supermodel promoting her line of cosmetics has for her proposition: "Buy my make-up system." She tends to avoid stating it, however, by showing her great beauty with the hope that such display will cause us to look favorably on her product and buy it. The political campaign speaker may have the proposition: "Vote for me," yet she tends to avoid such direct approach. Instead, she tries to gain favor by a discussion of the important problems that confront the nation or her constituents. Although in both these cases the audience is not unaware of the speaker's real proposition, neither the model nor the politician want to risk a negative reaction by too openly stating their proposition.

Debates

The proposition for a public debate should be carefully worded. Most usually it is stated formally as a resolution, such as "Resolved, that all peace proposals should be made under the auspices of the United Nations." Or, for publicity purposes, it may be stated less formally as a question, for example, "Should capital punishment be abolished?" A good debate proposition has two additional characteristics. It is worded in a complete sentence as an assertion and it places the burden of proof on the affirmative. The affirmative is the side that upholds the proposition; the negative opposes it. The affirmative will have the burden of proof if the proposition is so worded that it advocates a change from existing conditions. The affirmative must be for something new, something different.

Another way to determine whether the burden of proof is on the affirmative is to analyze the attitude of the audience toward the subject. The affirmative will have the burden of proof if the proposition is so worded as to be contrary to public opinion. In wording a proposition for public debate, be sure that it not only has the characteristics already described but is also a complete sentence and so phrased that the burden of proof falls on the shoulders of those who would support the proposition.

Public Discussions

The best type of proposition for discussion is one of policy. Propositions of fact or value may sometimes bring favorable results and be good topics for discussion; however, the proposition of policy is much more certain to bring strong participation. We call these "problem solution discussion questions." In public debate or advocacy, the proposition of policy is one that supports a particular course of action. The discussion question, however, should indicate a problem area and make possible the discussion of a variety of solutions. The debate proposition might be worded: "Resolved, that the developed nations should significantly reduce the use of fossil fuels." For discussion, the following wording might be used: "What are the best methods for limiting the use of fossil fuels?" In fact, the use of a single-solution kind of statement for discussion is unwise; the statement should be worded so that it allows a variety of solutions and so that the participants can make a choice among the various solutions available.

In summary, those who would influence by argument must carefully phrase propositions that they intend to advocate. These propositions may be of fact, value, or policy. Although the proposition is not always articulated in the speech, more frequently it is and appears at least as the final conclusion. The following are the characteristics of propositions that are worthy of argument:

1. I am interested in speaking on the proposition.

2. My audience will wish to hear me discuss the topic.

3. It is timely.

4. It is suitable for the occasion.

5. It is narrow enough to be covered within the time limits.

6. It is suitable for oral presentation.

7. It is subject to disagreement.

8. It is clear rather than ambiguous.

9. It is capable of being supported with evidence.

10. It is significant enough to be worthy of discussion.

11. It has a basis for comparison.

12. It involves a single topic.

EXERCISES

1. Define:
   a. Proposition
   b. Proposition of fact
   c. Proposition of value
   d. Proposition of policy
   e. The general purpose of a speech
   f. The specific purpose of a speech

2. Give examples of propositions of fact, value, and policy.

3. Bring to class a list of 10 propositions that would fulfill the tests of a good proposition.

4. Where would you look to find out what people are arguing about?
   a. Locally
   b. Within the state
   c. Nationally
   d. Internationally

5. The following is a list of propositions, some good, others lacking the characteristics of good propositions. First indicate the type of proposition and then apply the criteria to see if they are good subjects for argument:

a. Prejudice should be abolished.

b. It is better to have tried and failed than never to have tried at all.

c. Eisenhower was a greater general than Washington.

d. Subsidizing athletes is an immoral practice.

e. The Electoral College has been beneficial to the United States.

f. The writers of the European Union Constitution should have provided for a president to be selected by direct vote of the people.

g. Discrimination against homosexuals is a horrible practice.

h. Lincoln was a greater president than Washington.

i. George W. Bush should never have invaded Iraq.

j. Socrates should not have drunk hemlock, he should have made the Athenians execute him.

k. The civilization that came from Europe is better than any other.

l. The countries of the former Yugoslavia would be better off if they returned to socialism.

m. Truman was unjustified in using the atomic bomb on Japan during World War II.

n. Tobacco smoking causes cancer of the lungs.

o. European Union workers should not be allowed the right to strike.

p. Marriage counselors have been effective in preventing divorce.

q. Canada has a superior immigration policy than the United States.

r. The United States was justified in invading Afghanistan after the terrorist attacks of September 11, 2001.

Chapter 3
Analysis and Definition

So far we have considered the nature of argument and with what kinds of subjects it is effective. Our next step in the study of argument will be to learn to analyze and to define these subjects. We must know what we are talking about before we can influence others; thus, we must discover those arguments by which we can influence others. The purpose of this chapter is to help you develop a systematic way to understand a subject, to make the subject clear to others, and to discover the best arguments in the shortest time.

ANALYSIS DEFINED

Analysis may be defined as the process of discovering and understanding all the parts or all divisions of a subject and their interrelationships. To understand a watch, you would have to dismantle it to discover the parts and the subdivisions of the parts; you would probably also examine their operating interrelationship. The purpose of analysis in argumentation goes beyond mere understanding; it involves discovering the arguments available on the subject. In analysis, then, you should study a subject with a view to discover the best arguments to present to an audience. You should use the principles of analysis to make your audience understand what you are talking about.

Synthesis is the opposite of analysis. When you put the watch back together you are using the process of synthesis to restore the whole. A more common term for this process of synthesis by the public speaker or writer is *organization* or *outline*. In the process of organizing or outlining a particular speech or essay, however, you will seldom use all the parts of the subject, rather you will make a selection of the most convincing ones.

If you wish to write out all the parts of the subject for argument, you will employ the brief. The brief is a complete outline of all the arguments and all the evidence on a given subject. Lawyers getting ready for a court trial will make a brief of all the arguments and all the evidence pertinent to the case. This brief is a synthesis of what they have discovered. At the same time you analyze the subject, you will become concerned with the relationship of the parts; this relationship is called *arrangement*. After you have analyzed your material and wish to synthesize it into an outline form, you must be very careful to arrange the selected parts in the best order for influencing others.

Remember, analysis is the process of discovering the parts of a subject with the goal of studying it to discover the arguments available for influencing others. Analysis is not specific to the subject of argumentation but is equally important to exposition, to narration, and to other phases of persuasion. In fact, the process of studying any subject is the process of analyzing it. In writing term papers and examinations, you synthesize at least a part of what you have studied.

RULES FOR GOOD ANALYSIS

In analyzing a subject, you must be sure that you know the principles by which you are to divide your subject accurately.

Subdivide by One Principle

A set of coordinate headings will be properly interrelated because they have been chosen on this basis. The following list of parts of a tree is obviously faulty: sap, bark, branches, roots, pulp, leaves, and trunk. You can readily see that this division has been made on the basis of two principles: (1) by the constituent parts of the tree and (2) by its location in space. Reconsidering, you might divide the parts of a tree on the basis of location in space, in which case there would be four parts: the leaves, the branches, the trunk, and the roots. If subdivisions are needed or desired, the constituent elements of the leaves should be subdivided under that division and the same principle would be used to subdivide the other three parts. Likewise, in considering highways, you could not divide them by such headings as main highways, state highways, boulevards, alleys, secondary thoroughfares, and the like because you would be using two or more principles of division. Main, secondary, and tertiary thoroughfares are subdivided on the principle of amount of travel. Federal highways, state highways, and county highways are subdivided on the principle of their method of financial support. The terms *boulevards, alleys, avenues,* and so on are subdivided on the basis of types with only a partial relationship to the amount of use. Therefore, in your process of analysis, be sure to subdivide your topic by one principle.

Avoid Subdivisions that Overlap

When discussing the proposition, "The federal government should increase its subsidies for agricultural products," you will have some divisions that overlap if you use the following:

a. It would be good for workers.

b. It would be good for distributors.

c. It would be good for farmers.

d. It would be good for consumers.

The fourth division, consumers, overlaps the first three because the first three classes are all consumers. To discover whether your headings overlap, you can apply this test: Would the subdivisions under one heading appear again under a second or a third heading? If so, then they are overlapping. In the case above, the individuals who call themselves workers or distributors or farmers are also elements within the division of consumers. Sometimes, however, by refinement of your analysis you can avoid what at first would be overlapping. In the case above, rewording the headings as follows will avoid the overlapping:

a. It will stabilize the wages of farm workers.

b. It will reduce the problems of distributors.

c. It will assure income for farmers.

d. It will stop the inflation of prices for consumers.

Uncover All the Parts

Be sure, particularly in your preliminary study, that all phases of the topic have been uncovered. For example, you would fail to gain the belief of an audience "that a program of athletic scholarship should be adopted" if you only analyzed those arguments showing that it is needed. You must go on to articulate the arguments that will convince the audience that a system of athletic scholarships will actually produce athletic teams, that such system can meet expected costs, that establishing such a program won't be overwhelmingly difficult, and that no unusual problems will be encountered in raising the money. Many mistakes in history have been made because those who analyzed a situation failed to uncover all the parts. President Lyndon Johnson failed to understand the depth of the feeling of the Vietnamese people against his military actions. He failed to predict that the Vietnamese would fight a protracted guerilla war that would be difficult for America to win. Many believe that after World War II the Allies made mistakes in analysis when they gave the communists control of all the territory around Berlin. The failure to predict the grave difficulties that arose from this lack of access to the city brought repeated crises in the Cold War. Likewise, if your analysis is to be sound, you must not fail to uncover all the parts of the topic.

No Subdivision Should Equal the Whole Subject

This principle is fairly obvious, yet many fall into this error. A person might wish, for example, to subdivide the term *professional people* into:

- ministers
- lawyers
- teachers
- doctors
- people in the professions in general

The person analyzing this example realizes that she should uncover all the parts and knows that doctors, lawyers, ministers, and teachers are professional people, but she realizes that others are also classified as professional individuals. To be sure that she includes everybody, she puts in the fifth category to catch all of them. The moment she does, however, she falls into the fallacy of having one subdivision equaling the whole subject.

Utilize a Significant Principle

Analysis is basically a process of discovery. Sufficient study will show that almost any subject has subdivisions that belong there by the very nature of the subject. A person should not try to force on a given subject a type of subdivision that does not belong there by the nature of what is being studied. You will make the mistake of using an insignificant principle to divide a subject if you try, for example, to use a spatial principle of subdivision on a subject where space has no significance. The process of thinking, for instance, cannot be divided spatially because location in space has nothing to do with the process. We may use a spatial arrangement on the contributions of great thinkers, such as those from Greece, from Rome, or from Asia, but we can hardly use a spatial arrangement on types of reasoning. Many people try to overuse political, economic, social, cultural, educational, and religious areas when analyzing their subjects. This is a common way to subdivide activities, but this six-part subdivision can hardly be applied to such specific activities as playing football or skiing, even though both may have economic and social aspects. Using these sorts of subdivisions often creates wildly overlapping categories that fail to reveal important issues.

Be Sure that a Proper Interrelationship Among the Headings Is Present

Any subject has an inevitable interrelationship among its parts. This interrelationship must be discovered and the headings chosen must reveal it. A speech with unrelated headings will damage the prestige and credibility of its giver. Fallacies in this area are frequently found in those cases where an individual is searching for solutions to problems. Following is an example:

  a. Juvenile delinquency is on the increase.

  b. A significant cause of juvenile delinquency is a lack of parental guidance.

  c. We should see to it that young people have good recreational centers.

At first glance some relationship may seem to exist between the second and third headings; a closer analysis, however, reveals that if the cause is a lack of parental guidance, the only solution that would be properly related to that cause would be one that would provide sufficient guidance to make up for the deficiency. This mistake in analysis occurs frequently in proposals that suggest education as the solution. We hear people saying we should educate for democracy; we should educate to prevent illegal drug use; we should educate to stop crime. Education has only one goal and will overcome only one cause, and that is ignorance. Thus, those individuals who analyze problems and suggest education as a cure should make sure that the cause they are trying to remedy is ignorance. The good thinker will be careful to assure a proper relationship among the headings resulting from analysis.

Discovering the Main Issues

When individuals disagree on a proposition, an issue has been raised. We would therefore define an issue as a question that indicates the difference of opinion on a proposition. A second definition is that an issue is a question about which people may agree to disagree. An issue is stated in the form of a question and is a complete sentence. It also states the difference of opinion between two individuals or among groups. It is worded as a question so that it may be impartial, enabling both sides of the dispute to say, "Yes, that is the statement of our disagreement." Two of the important issues in the decision by the European Union and the United States to continue their high levels of agricultural subsidies are: (1) Do agricultural subsidies severely harm farmers in the majority of world nations? and (2) Are the internal political effects of discontinuing agricultural subsidies acceptable to American and European governments?

Wording issues clearly is extremely important. The superior speaker can word differences of opinion precisely and accurately in the form of a question. In a dispute, you should word your disagreement exactly in the form of an issue. Many disputants in social conversations, in public debates, and in personal disagreements often discover that they have no differences of opinion once they stop and word the issue. They find either that they are in agreement or else they are talking about two different things.

Definition of Main Issues

To influence belief on any proposition, certain chief issues must be established. Vital to gaining belief on a topic, these are called "main issues." Every proposition has within its inherent nature certain main issues that must be discovered. Let us consider a proposition and discover the main issues inherent within it.

Janet James is on trial for murder. What are the main issues that the prosecuting attorney must establish to determine her guilt? Here we turn to the legal definition of murder. A first-degree murderer may be defined as a human being who kills another with malice aforethought. The issues, then, involved in the case are as follows:

a. Was a human being killed?

b. Did Janet James do the killing?

c. Did Janet James have a developed plan for murdering this fellow human?

The prosecuting attorney must establish all three of these main issues and the belief of the jury must be gained on all three. The first issue can be established only if the prosecuting attorney can show that there is a dead body and that the death was the result of causes inflicted on the body by another human being. If this cannot be established, then the prosecuting attorney has no case.

Second, the prosecuting attorney must show that Janet James caused the death of the murdered person. If the defense attorney can show that someone else did it, or that some cause other than that produced by Janet James brought on the death, the case for the prosecution fails. Having established the first two, the prosecuting attorney must then proceed to prove that Janet James planned the murder. If Janet did it on the spur of the moment, she may be guilty, but not of first-degree murder. Thus, the prosecuting attorney must be able to establish all three of these main issues. Note that the defense attorney need only destroy or refute any one of the main issues to clear Janet of the charge of first-degree murder. Thus, the main issues of a particular proposition must be discovered and we must be able to establish all of them if we are to gain the belief of an audience on them.

The foregoing case is one that appears in law; main issues are equally important in other situations. Let us suppose the proposition is: "Should I apply for a job with the Gallagher Company?" At least four main issues are involved before you and your prospective employer agree that you should be hired for that particular job.

a. Do you have the training necessary to perform the job successfully?

b. Do you have the experience necessary for success?

c. Will the job pay sufficiently well for your services?

d. Is there opportunity for advancement?

The belief of both you and your prospective employer must be gained on each of those issues for you to be hired. If any one of them is answered "no," then you must look elsewhere. Thus you can see that every proposition has within it certain main issues that should be worded in question form so that the gaining of belief on the proposition requires a "yes" answer to each. One of the major tasks of analysis is to discover all the main issues necessary to gain belief on a proposition.

Analysis for Uncovering Subissues

Analysis is not only concerned with discovering main issues; it is also concerned with subordinate ones. Let us turn to the first issue of the last example: "Do I have the training necessary for success in the job?" The process of discovering the subordinate issues for that main issue is to develop criteria of the training for this particular job. You might decide on the following as your criteria:

a. Have I had sufficient general background courses?

b. Have I had sufficient specialized courses?

c. Have I developed the proper skills?

With such questions you would attempt to discover the proper subordinate issues and later use them as arguments to gain the belief on each of the main issues.

DISCOVERING MAIN ISSUES ACCORDING TO TYPE OF PROPOSITION

In Chapter 2 we learned that a person using an argument may focus on three types of propositions: fact, value, and policy. Each of these types of propositions has a special method of discovering the main issues.

Propositions of Fact

We have already indicated that courtroom trials are frequently concerned with propositions of fact. To discover the main issues of propositions of fact, we must know the definition of terms used in the statement. The prosecuting attorney in the example cited above has the job of trying to prove that Janet James is a murderer. To find the main issues by which she might prove her case, she must get the definition of a murderer. Out of the definitions within the statement she discovers her main issues. Study again the example cited above.

Here is still another proposition of fact. Suppose a prosecuting attorney must prove that Jim Johnson is a burglar. To do this he turns to the definition of a burglar and may readily discover the following: "A burglar is an individual who breaks into and enters a private dwelling at night with felonious intent." Having the definition before us we can then see that the prosecuting attorney must prove the following: (1) that Jim Johnson broke into, and (2) entered (3) a private dwelling (4) at night (5) with felonious intent. The main issues, then, are worded as follows:

a. Is the building with which we are concerned a private dwelling?

b. Was the private dwelling broken into?

c. Was the private dwelling entered?

d. Was the act committed at night?

e. Did Jim Johnson do it?

f. Did Jim Johnson commit this act with felonious intent?

Each of the six issues must be established to find Jim Johnson guilty of burglary. If he broke into and entered a building other than a private dwelling, he would be guilty of some crime but not burglary. If it happened in the daytime, he may be guilty of some other crime but not burglary. If a door were open and he walked in, he would not be guilty of burglary. All five of these must be established to gain belief on the proposition that the individual is a burglar. Note that the issues were discovered by finding the definition of the terms of the proposition, namely, the elements necessary in proving a person a burglar. These elements are then applied to the person involved.

Consider another example of a proposition of fact. Suppose you are trying to prove that "religious conservatism is on the increase in the United States." To find your issues you must define your terms and apply them on the basis of a significant time sequence. In doing so you would have to define religious conservatism. Having done this you would then proceed to make quantitative measurements at significantly selected periods of history, such as in the 1960s and in the late 1980s, and then note the particular increase in the 1990s. Additional notations would be necessary to bring your material up to date. In this way you would prove the increasing trend, if there is one, of religious conservatism in the United States. Thus, to discover the main issues of propositions of fact, you turn to the definition of terms.

Propositions of Value

A proposition of value is an assertion about the worth of a thing. To determine the worth of a thing, we use the process of evaluation, which applies criteria to the proposition. For example, to evaluate the following proposition, "Our college newspaper is a good one," we would establish the criteria of a good college newspaper. This would take considerable study of college newspapers, but we might come out with the following set of criteria:

- a. Does our college newspaper have a good system of administration?
- b. Does our college newspaper have good business management?
- c. Does our college newspaper report campus news effectively by both stories and pictures?
- d. Does our college newspaper have good feature articles?
- e. Does our college newspaper contain good editorials?
- f. Does our college newspaper have a good sports section?
- g. Does our college newspaper have a good system of training underclass students to take over positions of leadership?

By applying this set of criteria to your college newspaper, you will be able to evaluate its worth. For you to support this proposition, you would have to gain the belief of the audience on each of these to a degree sufficient for them to believe in your proposition. To prove the proposition a poor one, you would need merely prove that it falls down on a sufficient number of these factors. Thus, whenever you are working with propositions of value and trying to discover the main issues, you must establish a sound set of criteria by which the particular proposition can be measured. What these criteria are depends on the subject involved. In a newspaper, the area of journalism is involved; if you are discussing chain stores, then the principles of good retailing would be used. You can often find help in textbooks on the subject, which will usually provide you with guides to effective criteria for evaluation.

Propositions of Policy

Issues of propositions of policy are usually more extensive than propositions of fact and value. The main issues of propositions of policy are easier to discover because of the generalized wording of issues that serves as a guide for all of them. Propositions of policy are concerned first of all with the bad things within the present system. After these evils are uncovered and their causes found, the next step is to find a solution for them. This solution then becomes a new system or a modification of the old whereby the evils will be removed. The following questions indicate the main issues in propositions of policy:

a. Are evils caused by the present system?

b. Are these evils great enough to demand a change?

c. Are the evils inherent and impossible to repair in the present system?

d. Will the proposed solution remove the evils?

e. Is the proposed solution free from objections?

f. Is the proposed solution the best?

Let us apply these for a moment to a proposition of policy. If our proposition is: "The federal government should establish a system of government-sponsored medical insurance in the United States," these generally worded questions would produce the following:

a. Is there a need to change our present method of paying medical bills?

   (1) Does our present system of paying for medical care have evils?

   (2) Are those evils great enough to warrant a change in our system of payment?

   (3) Is it impossible to improve our method of payment without changing to a new system?

b. Is a system of government-sponsored medical insurance practical?

   (1) Will the system of government-sponsored medical insurance remove the evils?

   (2) Will government-sponsored medical insurance be sufficiently free from objections?

   (3) Is government-sponsored medical care the best solution?

Notice that these questions are the vital issues in gaining the belief of an audience on the subject and we must be able to gain belief on all of them because they are the main issues of that proposition. By utilizing these questions, a debater may discover the vital issues on propositions of policy. There may be other wordings to these questions, but they will be similar enough for our purposes. For example, you may run onto such wordings as: "Is the new proposal advantageous?" or, "Is the new proposal workable?" The questions listed under point a above may be lumped into one wording: "Is there a need for a change?" Starting with these, you must proceed to find the subpropositions of fact in the form of evils in the present system and then go on to find the supposed advantages or at least the evils that the new solution will remove.

Stock Issues and Stock Ways of Dividing Subjects

Analysis is one of the big problems confronting the thinking person. To divide subjects into their proper parts without committing fallacies is no easy task. Many methods are available to subdivide topics of all kinds. Those who engage in this work have developed what are called "stock" issues and "stock" ways of dividing subjects into their parts.

What are stock issues? They are general statements of issues that will apply to a broad category of subjects of the same type. Stockrooms contain supplies that we use when they are needed. Stock issues, then, become the means by which we supply ourselves with issues on propositions of the same category. Thus, the general statements of the main issues of propositions of policy, discussed above, are the stock issues of propositions of policy and will apply to all propositions of policy.

Stock ways are available to you when you wish to either subdivide or arrange subjects; you may wish to draw from them to help you analyze either a subject or a proposition.

Chronological

This method divides subjects on the basis of time sequence, that which happened first being placed first and that which happened last being placed last. Historians writing on the United States have rather universally used the same divisions of history. This frequent division is:

Worlds Meet

Colonization and Settlement

The Revolution and the New Nation

Expansion and Reform

Civil War and Reconstruction

The Development of the Industrial United States

The Emergence of Modern America

The Great Depression and World War II

Postwar United States

Contemporary United States

Thus, when considering those subjects that involve a time sequence, you may turn to the stock chronological way of dividing it. For example, the chronological method can be used to discover the main divisions of making things, such as baking a cake. Here, you would use that method to divide your subject into its main parts. The chronological method can be valuable in discovering the main issues or subordinate issues of a proposition. Let us say your proposition is: "There is a trend toward religious conservatism in the United States." Since you are discussing it, you might wish to make either your main or your subordinate issues periods or eras of time within the history of the country. We recommend that you develop skill in the use of stock chronological divisions, so that you have a variety of these readily available when you need them.

Spatial

A second stock way of dividing subjects is by using arrangements in space. In an analysis of trees, the divisions might be made on a spatial basis. Using that arrangement, you would arrive at the leaves, the branches, the trunk, and the roots. Subjects related to geography often lend themselves to spatial arrangement. The baseball teams of the American League could be arranged according to a spatial method starting with the team that is the farthest east and proceeding to one that is the farthest west. We have a stock way of dividing the world by continents; the stock way of dividing the United States—the New England states, the Middle Atlantic states, the Southern states, the Midwestern states, the Southwestern states, the Mountain states, and the Western states. We have stock ways of dividing buildings on the basis of spatial arrangement, starting with the basement or foundation and proceeding upward to the roof. Analyzing by arrangement in space is a process, then, of moving from east to west, or north to south, or of starting at the top and going to the bottom, or starting from the bottom and going to the top. For many subjects this is a meaningful way to divide them and to arrive at the main divisions or the main issues.

Topical

As we analyze them, some subjects do not seem to have any particular type of arrangement of their parts. There is neither time sequence nor a spatial relationship; there seems to be no problem-solution or cause-to-effect relationship. With such subjects, therefore, we often use what may be called a "topical" division. Usually in a topical division, little difference is apparent in the ordering of the main division, which comes first and which comes second is irrelevant, but certain stock or usual methods of dividing the subject do exist. For example, in analyzing a particular era or period, historians may use the stock topical divisions of political, economic, social, religious, educational, and cultural phases of the life of the time they are studying.

In school you have probably become aware that authors of textbooks make great use of topical arrangement of subjects. The student of botany is quite aware that the types of trees are arranged on a topical basis. Frequently they are divided into families and then the various members of the family are listed in no particular order. The chemist will make use of topical arrangement in suggesting the qualities of a particular element. Sometimes a factor may be introduced, such as weight, to determine the order in which the elements themselves are studied. In other words, some modification of the topical arrangement may be made on the basis of some principle.

Psychological

The public speaker or writer is quite aware of the fact that various materials that she may have within her speech or essay may have more impact on some of her listeners or readers than on others. A subject that at first seems to be topical may with further study appear to be better arranged psychologically. A psychological arrangement is one in which the strongest point is put first, then the least strong is put next, and the rest of the speech constructed so that the second strongest comes last. Inasmuch as audiences are frequently difficult to win, the strongest possible arguments should be placed first in an attempt to get a favorable initial hearing. The rest of the speech then is built on a climactic order so that the speech ends with strength. Note that topical arrangement should always be scrutinized with a view to discovering whether the psychological approach would be preferable. Although this particular principle is utilized more often with subjects demanding topical analysis, it may also be used with the other forms of analysis. Storytellers often start with an exciting moment and then flash back to the beginning and bring the listener up to date.

Determining which of the points or arguments is strongest can be difficult. At least two factors should be considered when you are making such determination. One, the emotional appeal on which the argument or the point is based. Those arguments resting on the strongest basic wants tend to be more compelling. Humankind fights for freedom of speech and freedom of the press. Thus, an argument based on these will often be very persuasive.

Another way to determine the strength of an argument is to discover how much support material is available to develop it. Arguments for which the evidence is overwhelming tend to be more powerful than those that have a great deal of doubt associated with them. Ordinarily those main headings developed with excellent human interest stories or great amounts of support material tend to be strong. Thus, those arguments that have both strength in the amount of support material and the power to touch the emotions of the listener will tend to be the strongest.

Logical

Subjects can be divided on the basis of logical arrangement. Propositions of fact and propositions of value will frequently be divided on the basis of any of the four foregoing methods: chronological, spatial, topical, or psychological. Propositions of policy, however, will utilize the logical arrangement almost exclusively in handling the main issues. Questions of policy will utilize the stock problem-solution issues outlined above. The six that were given in discussing the main issues of propositions of policy are probably the best for the purposes of those who would present arguments.

Other stock ways of dividing propositions of policy are available, as are other forms of that type of analysis known as "logical." One of these is John Dewey's formula for problem solving. Dewey's analysis of reflective thinking revolves around the following five fairly distinctive phases:

a. Recognition of a felt difficulty

b. Location and definition of the problem

c. Description of representative hypotheses or solutions of the problem

d. Rational elaboration of these suggestions and the testing of each

e. Experiment and verification leading to acceptance or rejection of the preferred solution

Note how closely these are related to the stock issues mentioned in the earlier section. If you were interested in a well-organized problem-solution discussion, such a division of your question would constitute a good choice. Some may find it complicated and wish to simplify it. If so it can be reduced to the following:

1. What is the problem and how serious is it?

2. What are the various solutions, with the advantages and disadvantages of each?

3. What is the best solution?

Those three steps will be satisfactory for the discussion of most topics. Sometimes you might wish to add a fourth, "What are the best methods of implementing the chosen solution?" So helpful are these stock ways of dividing a discussion subject that we recommend that you drill yourself in their use and learn to use them well.

Are other modifications of the method of logical analysis available? Yes; one is to think first of the causes and then search for the effects. In this reasoning pattern the causes will be given first and the effects of those causes second. Or the process may be reversed—you have observed certain effects and then you proceed to uncover the causes. Solutions are often discussed by this method. The solution is described and the causal force that it contains is explained. This then is followed by a description of the good effects that derive from the solution. The causal force and its adverse effects are countered by the solution. Economic downturns have often been discussed on the basis of elaborating the effects first and then attempting to discover the causes. This method may help both your analysis and your later synthesis of a subject you are interested in.

Still another type of logical analysis or arrangement is known as the "method of residues" or the "this or nothing" method. The use of this method is to suggest four to six answers to questions or a variety of solutions to a problem. Discuss each and show how it is false or poor and then finally end with one that is not perfect but is the only one left. This is called "method of residues" and results from it being the residual solution. It is "this or nothing." You may find this to be the most effective method for synthesizing your speech. Utilize this method to disarm your audience and to make them realize that this is as good a solution as you can discover.

In the section of this chapter in which we have explained stock issues and stock ways of dividing subjects, please remember that the principles are applicable not only to subjects utilizing argument but to other subjects as well. These are the principles of division of any subject. Issues, however, pertain only to those subjects in which there is disagreement, only to those subjects in which argument is used. Remember that chronological, spatial, topical, and psychological divisions may be used to determine the issues involved in questions of fact or value. Questions of policy in which you desire to gain belief on a new proposal utilize the stock method of logical division. In discussion, although the questions may have the appearance of issues to be utilized in gaining belief, they are actually used more for the purpose of gaining understanding.

DEFINITION

One of the steps in analyzing a topic is definition. The purpose of definition is to gain an understanding, to make something clear. It is an art to be able to define things well and fortunately numerous methods of definition are available to anyone using argument.

Logical Definition

A logical definition involves three steps:

    a. Name the thing to be defined

    b. Put it into a class or category

    c. Set it off from all other members of the class or category

For example, if you wished to give a logical definition of analysis, you would use the following three steps:

    a. Analysis is

    b. a process

    c. of discovering all parts of a subject.

Because the formulation of a good definition is so important to the thought process, you must be able to test each definition to make sure that it is precise. The three steps mentioned above give us three of the four tests by which we can test our definition. The first test is whether we have named what is to be defined; the second test is whether the class or category into which we put the object is a valid one. In our definition of analysis above, we might do better to put analysis into the category of a thought process. Many people, including students, make their definitions inferior by utilizing the words *when* and *where*. Avoid definitions that begin "analysis is when . . ." or "analysis is where . . ." The third test of a good definition is whether the thing to be defined has been set off from all other members of the class or category. "Public speaking is that process in which ideas are imparted to others" is fallacious because it does not set public speaking apart from other forms of communication, such as writing, which also may be used to impart ideas to others. Any definition then that fails to separate the thing being defined from all other members of the class or category is fallacious. The fourth test of a logical definition is whether the definition includes all members of the class or category that is being defined. Often deductive reasoning is defined as "that reasoning process in which one goes from the general to the specific." This is a poor definition because not all forms of deductive reasoning are included. At best this is only somewhat descriptive of categorical deduction and fails to include the other two types, disjunctive and hypothetical. The only sound definition of deduction covers all types of deduction. (See Chapter 7 on deduction for the actual definition.) Thus, in giving a good logical definition, be sure that all types or all parts of the subject being defined are included in the process of defining it. By applying these four tests to your definition as you take an examination, give a speech, or write a term paper, you can make sure that you are on firm ground.

Definition by Example

Using an example is one of the best ways to make clear what you are talking about. It has been said, "An illustration is a window in the argument letting in light." The example or illustration is a story about your idea. To define by example, you apply the things to be defined to specific cases. Want to cite an example of how the parliamentary form of government works? Tell the story of what has happened in Canada or some other nation that uses the system. In fact, we suggest that the most effective way to define in an examination, in a speech, or in an essay is to give the logical definitions first and then follow with examples of the things cited. You will notice that in writing this book, the authors used this method extensively.

Definition by Comparison

The unknown is understood only on the basis of past experiences. If a person has never experienced the thing being defined, she will be unable to get a picture unless she can associate it with some experience similar to it in the past. Definition by comparison is the method in which the unknown is compared with something familiar. To describe an airplane to someone who has never seen one is difficult unless you can compare the structure of the airplane with that of a bird. The listener, having seen a bird, can then understand what is meant by the wings and the fuselage of the plane as it is being compared with a bird.

Definition by Contrast

Closely related to definition by comparison is definition by contrast. An individual wishing to give a picture of an airplane to someone who has never seen one probably would not stop with comparison. He would also have to point out the differences—in the form of the stationary wing, in thrust of the jet engine as contrasted with the flapping of the wings of the bird. Comparison and contrast are often used to shed light on current happenings or in predicting future happenings by comparing and contrasting them to old and familiar events.

Definition by Synonym

This method is similar to comparison. A strange or unknown word is explained in terms of familiar words that have approximately the same meaning. For example, you might try to explain stuttering by using the phrase "blocking in speech." By using a more familiar word the idea is made simpler or clearer. Often speakers make use of the established device of using three synonyms so that not only will the idea be made clear but emphasis can be achieved. Consider the following sentence: "He will become a great man; he will become a Washington, a Lincoln, a Jefferson." Note that the specific names are virtually synonymous with the term *great man,* yet citing the three makes the picture more concrete and increases the effectiveness of the idea being presented.

Definition by Etymology or Origin

A debater defines by etymology when she traces a word back to its original language and translates it in terms of that original meaning. The word *psychology* came from the Greek words *psyche,* meaning "the mind" or "the soul," and *ology,* meaning "the study of." Thus, the original meaning of the word psychology was the study of the mind or soul. *Schizophrenia* comes from two Greek words—*schizo* meaning a "split" or "division" and *phrenia,* which comes from the word *phren* meaning "mind" or "heart." Thus, schizophrenia according to etymology means a "mental illness characterized by a split mind or heart." Definition by etymology is available for your use and is often an effective way to make meaning clear.

Definition by Negation

Words having many meanings often need accurate classifications. Often one defines what a thing is by telling what it is not. This is called "definition by negation." The term *socialism* has so many differing meanings that if you wish to use it you should say exactly what you mean and what you do not mean by it. Thus, if you mean government ownership and operation of basic industries, you must make very clear in your definition that, as you are using the term *socialism*, you do not mean social security, you do not mean ownership and operation of retail stores, you do not mean prepaid medical care. Then you should end your definition by saying what you do mean. You may do it by saying something like this: "By *socialism* I do not mean social security, I do not mean government ownership and operation of retail stores, I do not mean prepaid medical care. By *socialism* I mean government ownership and operation of such basic industries as manufacturing, mining, transportation, and public utilities." Definition by negation is particularly valuable in defining complex terms.

Definition by Enumeration or Division

One way to make clear what you are talking about is to enumerate the parts of the subject or term. For instance, the term *basic industries* is rather ambiguous; at least it is not clear to many people just what industries are involved. Thus, as in the example above, you can define the basic industries by enumerating them: the mining industries, the transportation industries, and public utilities industries. By such enumeration you make clear just what you are talking about. Consider another example. It is difficult to give a logical definition of the term *logical definition*. You will find that by enumerating the parts of it, you will be able to make the term much clearer. Thus you enumerate part one, which is naming the thing to be defined, then part two, which is putting it into a class, and then part three, which is setting it off from other members of the class. Enumeration of the parts can simplify the process of giving a logical definition.

Definition by Authority

Often you will wish to give support to the particular definition you use. Particularly this is essential when the definition you give a term may cause a dispute. Thus, if you are going to use the term *globalization* in public debate or discussion and expect some dispute over its exact meaning, you should turn to authorities in the fields of political science and economics to see how they define the term. In this way you may justify your own definition. Definition by authority, then, is using the logical definition and stating the name of the authority that has phrased it. In speaking the usual form is: "Professor X defines *globalization* as...."

Definition by History

Sometimes the easiest way to define a particular concept is to go back and trace not only its origin but also the evolution by which it came to have its present meaning. Probably as easy a way as any to define the Monroe Doctrine is to give its origin and to briefly trace the history of its use. In so doing, you can quite properly and effectively point out certain significant features of that history that shed additional light on your interpretation. Understanding communism is difficult unless you go back to the theories of Karl Marx and their application in the twentieth century by Vladimir Lenin and Josef Stalin, Mao Zedong, and others.

We have enumerated and discussed 10 different ways by which you can define a word, a term, or a concept. Actually, the logical definition is the one true way to define. The other nine are merely aids to definition. Thus, in using argument, you should define basic terms so that no misunderstanding ensues and so that disputes can be avoided. The speaker or writer in using argument may wish to add clarity to his meaning. In that case, he will turn to any of the additional aids to definition to make certain that his listeners or readers understand thoroughly. Each of these methods of definition has great value at particular times and the choice of the proper one or more will bring the most effective results. Drilling in their use will be time well spent.

THE STEPS IN PRELIMINARY ANALYSIS

Now that we have discussed some of the more important features of analysis and definition, we will go on to develop an organized method of approaching any subject about which we wish to present arguments. Following are examples of the preliminary steps for analyzing a topic:

+ Determine the immediate cause for discussion of the topic
+ Define clearly the various terms to be used
+ Develop a brief history of the proposition or subject
+ Outline the various factors of universal agreement covered by the proposition. What are the common areas of agreement that you can assume?
+ Make a statement of the main issues involved in the propositions

The last four of these steps have been explained earlier in this chapter. Here we are going to take up the first point—the immediate cause for discussion (reasons why the issue should be talked about at this particular time). Causes for discussion may be that an international, national, state, or local government unit is going to have to consider a new law, or that the newspapers and periodicals have been printing articles about it, or that some special event has taken place or will take place that demands our thinking about it. Thus, the first step in the preliminary analysis of a topic would be the listing of those reasons why it is both significant and timely for this particular audience.

These five steps, arranged in this order, will allow you to start studying any subject. Often in developing a speech or an essay on a proposition for which you wish to present arguments, you will use these five steps to get the hearer or reader to understand what you are talking about. Some have said that argument consists of two things: the statement of the proposition about which you are going to present your arguments and the presentation of arguments for it. These five steps are used in performing the first task.

COMPLETE OR CONTINUING ANALYSIS

Is there any subject that we can confidently say that all possible investigation has been done? Almost certainly not. As time passes, we discover new ideas and additional information about many things. The insurance salesperson analyzes insurance for a long period. Yet time brings many changes. Changing conditions demand new services, so the good insurance salesperson continues to analyze how insurance can serve the public better. At one time the atom seemed to be the final analytical unit of an element. Not satisfied, however, that this was the end of the investigation, scientists discovered that the atom could be split. This continuing analysis brought us the beginning of the Atomic Age. Congress and legislatures have found that laws that were once probably good become unjust or outmoded with time. Thus, our laws on discrimination have been changed and amended, and we can expect more changes. The law that is just under today's conditions may be unjust with tomorrow's events. The study of human beings has been going on for centuries. We know much more now than we once did, but the final analysis has never been made and perhaps never will be. Accordingly, we must make as complete an analysis as we can at the moment and then continue.

ANALYSIS IN READING, LISTENING, WRITING ESSAYS, AND WRITING EXAMINATIONS

This textbook is primarily intended for the speaker who desires to influence others by using argument. The principles of this chapter on analysis, however, have an application far beyond the speaker using argument. Before we complete our chapter, then, we would like to give you a few suggestions that may be of value in developing your skill in reading, listening, writing essays, and writing examinations.

Reading

Most authors who have written articles or books have analyzed their subjects and have then synthesized their material in the form of an outline. The first step that you should take in reading a book aimed at explaining some subject is to discover the author's outline. First, read the preface. The whole outline will not be uncovered there, but clues as to the intention of the author can be discovered. Next, turn to the table of contents for the list of chapter headings. Often you will notice that the analysis of the author has led her to divide the book into parts with chapters as subdivisions. Having perused this bird's-eye view, then turn to particular chapters to discover the author's outline by reading the topic headings. Take care to notice which ones are main topics and which are subordinate. Look at topic sentences of paragraphs to discover the author's complete outline of the chapter, although some authors may print the outline of the chapter at its beginning. Having thus discovered the outline of each chapter, you are ready to glean detailed information from your reading.

Listening

When you listen to a lecture or a speech, the foregoing method cannot be used to discover the outline of the speaker. The result is that most of us hear a lecture and get little beyond a general impression. We are unable to remember or evaluate the details of the speaker's argumentative processes or the details by which she makes her subject clear. The only way that this can be done is to outline the speech. Use pencil and paper and watch for the following:

- What portion of the speech is the introduction?
- Does she utilize any of the five steps of preliminary analysis?
- What are her main headings?
- Does she have main headings followed by subordinate headings?

- What support material did she use to develop each main heading?
- What support material did she use to develop any subordinate headings?
- What portion of her speech was the conclusion?

At first this may be difficult, but with increased familiarity with the above and with practice, you will find taking notes much easier.

Writing Essays

Many of the principles described in this chapter on analysis apply equally well to writing essays. You should: use the preliminary steps in analysis; discover the main divisions of your subject; discover the subdivisions of your subject. At the same time you should be ready to define terms as necessary. The stock ways to divide subjects into their parts may be of great value in helping you discover the parts. Obviously, you should observe those rules that help you determine whether your analysis is a good one. Thus we suggest that everything you learn in this text about analysis can be applied to writing. Stylistic elements will differ, however—you will not repeat so often in essays nor will you necessarily be so direct in your language.

Writing Examinations

Use the skills described in this chapter when taking examinations, particularly when you are called on to answer essay questions. It might bring you a distinctly better grade. Many examinations require you to "define" or "discuss." In those questions requesting a definition, be sure to observe the recommendation that you use a logical definition and that you apply the four tests to see if your definition is a good one. Find out ahead of time whether your instructor likes a one sentence logical definition or wishes you to expand your definition to include the logical one plus one of the additional aids to definition. Whenever a question requires you to discuss a topic, consider whether you should divide the question into parts and then answer part one, part two, part three, part four, and so on. Often in a discussion question you should define the concepts suggested, combining the logical definition with a definition by example. Then you can proceed to discuss each of the various parts of the subject should you decide that it is required. We suggest additional aids in this chapter that you might use from time to time on an essay examination. Being able to define your terms and divide your answers into parts are valuable skills. Those who use good methods of analysis always leave the impression of being good thinkers.

Exercises

1. Define the following terms:
   a. Analysis
   b. Issues
   c. Main issues
   d. Subordinate issues
   e. Stock issues
   f. Chronological arrangement
   g. Spatial arrangement
   h. Topical arrangement
   i. Psychological arrangement
   j. Logical arrangement
2. Explain each of the six rules for good analysis.
3. Why would the violation of any one of the six rules for good analysis be called "fallacies in analysis"?
4. How are the main issues of propositions of fact discovered?
5. How are the main issues for questions of value discovered?
6. How are the main issues for propositions of policy discovered?
7. Explain each of the following stock ways of dividing subjects:
   a. Chronological
   b. Spatial
   c. Topical
   d. Psychological
   e. Logical
8. Why can the five stock ways of dividing subjects as indicated in Exercise 7 be considered both stock ways of analyzing subjects and stock ways of arranging subjects?

9. Choose a general subject—space exploration, computer-assisted learning, or Internet file sharing of music and video, for example—and analyze various aspects of the subjects by using chronological, spatial, topical, psychological, and logical methods of division. Apply the rules for good analysis to avoid any fallacies in your analysis. Be sure your example is one that would be effective were you to use it in class or with some other audience.

10. Using some general subject as suggested in Exercise 9, illustrate each of the ten ways by which you can define a concept. Let the concept be the subject itself or some phase within that more general topic.

11. Utilizing that same general topic or one similar to it, work out the preliminary steps of analysis, and

    a. Write them out to be handed in

    b. Prepare to report orally on them to the class

12. Discuss what is meant by complete or continuing analysis and why is it important?

13. What specific recommendations concerning the principles of analysis would you give to those who

    a. Read

    b. Listen

    c. Write examinations

    d. Write essays

14. What principles of division (rules for good analysis) are violated in the following?

    a. Brook trout

        Salmon trout

        Rainbow trout

        Lake trout

    b. Lawyers believe it

        Physicians believe it

        Teachers believe it

        Professional people in general believe it

c. Passenger boats

   Sailboats

   Yachts

   Steamboats

   Freighters

d. Authoritarian nations adhere to it

   Neutral nations adhere to it

   Democracies adhere to it

e. Economic aspects of skiing

   Social aspects of skiing

   Political aspects of skiing

   Cultural aspects of skiing

f. Men's service clubs favor it

   Parent-teacher organizations favor it

   Youth groups favor it

   Membership groups favor it

g. Oak trees

   Hardwood trees

   Pine trees

   Softwood trees

   Maple trees

h. Alcohol being served at our college parties

   at our college banquets

   at our college dates

   at our college social life in general

i. Trees consist of leaves

   branches

   and trunks

j. Roof

Furnace

Foundation

Fireplace

Walls

k. Passenger cars

Compact cars

SUVs

Vans

Delivery vehicles

l. Economic aspects of automobiles

Political aspects of automobiles

Social aspects of automobiles

Cultural aspects of automobiles

Educational aspects of automobiles

m. Farmers believe in it.

Lawyers believe in it

Businessmen believe in it

Professional people believe in it

15. List the main issues essential to gaining belief of the audience of each of the following propositions:

a. Tom Jones is an armed robber. (Assume that the legal definition of an armed robber is a person who takes the property of another under the threat of a lethal weapon.)

b. This old house is a good one. (Assume for this question that a good house is one that has been constructed well, has been maintained well, has good plumbing facilities, good heating facilities, well planned layout of rooms, and windows adequate for ventilation and light.)

c. Our university should adopt the honor system for examinations.

d. Sam Smith is a murderer. (Assume the legal definition of a murderer to be a person who kills another with malice aforethought.)

e. Our university is an excellent university. (Assume that an excellent university is one that has good buildings, good grounds, adequate space, excellent teaching facilities, a good curriculum, excellent teachers, a good library, and a good administrative staff.)

f. John Jones is a shoplifter. (Assume the legal definition of a shoplifter to be a person who takes articles from a retail store without the owner's consent during business hours and has no intention of paying for them.)

g. Our school paper is a good one. (Assume that a good college newspaper is one that has a good system of administration, good business management, reports campus news effectively by both stories and pictures, has good feature articles, good editorials, and a good system of training underclass students to take over positions of leadership.)

Chapter 4
Gathering Material for Building Arguments

If you are really concerned with influencing the belief and conduct of others on any subject, get the best information you can to assure success. This information consists of the arguments you choose and the materials you use to support your arguments. Gathering good material will not only help you analyze the subject so that you may arrive at the best selection of arguments but also provide documentation of your facts. In this chapter we shall address how to gather material in the least possible time and with a minimum of effort.

NECESSITY OF AN ORGANIZED SYSTEM OF GATHERING MATERIAL

Sometimes a prospective speaker will go to an article in a current magazine and make that article into a speech. This happens all too often in the college classroom. Nothing could be worse. Your own ideas and your personal intent are far more valuable to you than the ideas of other people. Or you might read a couple of articles and maybe even two or three books on the subject. Certainly this is better, but books and articles are written from a particular point of view, so you may see only one side of the picture and your analysis of the whole subject will be far from complete. Rather than reading (and taking on) others' opinions, you should develop a systematic plan to gather materials that will accomplish two objectives. First, the materials you gather should make possible a complete analysis of the subject. You will want to become aware of all sides and many points of view, if possible. As you discover how opinions vary about your subject, you will be able to plan your speech to lead your listeners in the direction you intend. Your second objective will be to gather the support material that will constitute the evidence on which you base your arguments. Your gathered material will supply the facts you will use to change the opinions of your listeners. You will want to find those examples, those statistics, and those opinions of authorities that will best support your selected argument. With these two objectives in mind, let's lay out an organized plan for gathering material.

Importance of Your Own Knowledge and Thinking

Those propositions or subjects that are best for you to choose are those with which you have had the most direct experience or that interest you most. If you become a corporation president in the computer industry, almost inevitably the main subject that you will talk about will be computers, peripherals, and software. The insurance executive mentioned earlier will inevitably speak on insurance because she has had more experience with it than anything else. In your life, you have had more direct experiences with certain subjects or propositions than others. Furthermore, you probably have more knowledge and have thought more about unfamiliar subjects than you give yourself credit for at first. Don't sell yourself short.

To gather the maximum from your own knowledge and thinking, you should make a preliminary analysis of the subject. On a sheet of paper:

1. List all the causes for discussion.

2. Outline briefly pertinent facts of the history of the problem.

3. Define the terms in your own words.

4. List all the arguments (pay strong attention to this step) you can think of on the proposition. If it is a proposition of policy, for example, list all the evils or disadvantages that might constitute the need for a new policy. Then proceed to think out in detail the solution or various solutions that you have in mind. Then list all the arguments supporting the adoption of that solution. Note that these are only lists of arguments and you should anticipate that further study might cause you to change your mind about the strength of each.

5. List all the facts that you already know to support your arguments. Make a list for each heading or premise. Pay particular attention to good factual examples that can be used later in the speech. Often your choice of one argument over another will be determined by the strength of the support material you can find in the form of examples and statistics.

The results of making the preliminary analysis solely on the basis of your own knowledge and thinking will often astonish you. You will find that you know far more about a particular subject than you would have believed. Furthermore, on subjects with which you have had a lot of experience you may need go no further in gathering material than to check the accuracy of your facts. Such an organized program carried out before you proceed any further in your gathering of material will save you a lot of time and will result in a stronger speech.

EXCHANGING OPINIONS AND KNOWLEDGE WITH OTHERS

Your first inclination on approaching any subject, even before you make your own preliminary analysis, may be to go immediately to the library. More important, however, even after going through the preliminary analysis, is to exchange opinions and knowledge with others.

Discussion

You should discuss your topic with members of your family, your roommates, and your friends. In these informal discussions, members of your own family and friends will reveal to you what attitudes various members of your audience will have toward your subject. You will learn where they will agree and disagree. You will discover on what arguments you will have to muster strong evidence to change opinions. Furthermore, your friends may have factual examples to help you support some of your arguments. Likewise, you will find what particular arguments and what facts tend to be influential. In informal discussion you can virtually test all parts of a speech before giving it.

Personal Interviews

Material gathered through an interview with some authority in a field will aid considerably. Some of our students, wishing to speak on the subject of crime, drove to the office of the State Police. They found those law enforcement professionals quite ready and eager to give them facts and information about crime within the state. Furthermore, the statistics gathered from the files of the State Police were not available in any library and they were up to date. Another student, wishing to speak on water pollution, visited the city engineer's office as the only means of discovering how seriously the water in the lake and river was polluted and what was being done about it. The actual experience of visiting the city engineer brought an excitement to the subject as it was revealed to the audience. Therefore, when possible, we suggest personal interviews with individuals whose daily lives are concerned with the proposition you are advocating.

Letters and E-mail

When particular information is needed and a personal interview is out of the question, try to gather information by writing either to authorities in the field or to people working in the area with which your proposition is concerned. Writing letters and sending e-mail is preferred only when you desire a specific bit of information. Do not abuse this method. For example, don't write a letter or e-mail saying, "I have a speech to give on such and such a topic. Would you please send me any information and thoughts you have on it?" Rather, write asking for specific information, particularly in the form of factual data; for instance you might ask a city official to send you the crime rate for specific categories for the previous year. Thus, letters constitute a good source of specific, but not of general, data.

Thus, informal discussion, personal interviews, and letters will be helpful in gathering materials for analysis, for understanding the audience, and for obtaining good support material.

OBSERVATION

Observation is a means of gathering material by direct experience, which furnishes the most vivid information for your speech. We know vividly what we have seen, heard, smelled, and touched, and it is easier to picture it to others. Some high school students became interested in the subject of hydroelectric power as a replacement for fossil fuels. Fortunately for them, both a hydroelectric power plant and a gas-fired power plant were located near their town. They made appointments to be shown through the plants and saw water and gas turbines. They observed how these were connected with the huge dynamos that generated electricity. They used a map to trace the way electricity was distributed in the region and along the national power grid. This was an exciting day for them, and, when they discussed the subject of hydroelectricity throughout the following months, they knew what they were talking about when they used the words *gas turbines* and *water turbines*. They also became aware of the ecological problems inherent in hydroelectric facilities because they learned that the migration of fish had been disturbed and ecosystems had been flooded when the facility was built. We can so easily fall into the habit of going only as far as the library or the Internet and neglecting one of the greatest sources of information, namely, a plant or a business operating right in our own community. A student was once asked, after giving a speech on fast food restaurants, where he gathered his material. His answer, "Why, at the library, of course." When the professor asked him, "Why didn't you visit fast food restaurants, comparing prices with the more traditional lunch counters, comparing general attractiveness and similar features?" the student answered, "I never thought of that." How much more compelling his speech would have been had he done so. Thus, if you are going to talk on crime, visit the courts in your community. If you are going to talk on labor-management relations, sit in on labor union meetings, go to a plant, and see people's working conditions. Often you will have vivid experiences that you can use in your speech.

CONDUCTING ORIGINAL EXPERIMENTS AND RESEARCH

Some of the best support material that you can gather to influence belief is that which you determine for yourself. Material gathered by direct experiment often becomes more real for you and thus you can use and picture it more effectively. For example, if you are trying to impress the audience with the argument that one should experience bungee-jumping as an extreme sport, you can gather significant materials on your own. Have various friends actually try bungee-jumping and then interview them. You can then ask them to compare it with other thrilling activities, such as white-water rafting. Your use of material that you gather directly from your friends will add weight and impressiveness to your attempt to gain your audience's belief. You might even try it yourself. Furthermore, the reactions of your friends in trying the activity will be available for comment; such primary material is difficult to find elsewhere. Thus, the description of their experiences will be more attention-getting than statistics from a book. Consider another example: You are trying to develop an argument that a poem should be learned as a complete unit rather than stanza by stanza. You may find evidence for this argument from psychology books. Nevertheless, describing an experiment you conducted asking some of your friends to learn the material stanza by stanza and others by complete units will add vividness. You can use a watch to time the process of memorizing. The contrasting results will be much more alive and meaningful than a quotation from a book. A student in one of our classes wished to reinforce the argument that the cost of shaving with an electric razor was less than with a safety razor. He conducted a survey of the members in his fraternity to see how much they spent annually on lotions, soaps, and safety razors. By using material that he gathered he made his argument more believable. The result was that he sold not only the members of the class but his instructor as well. The foregoing are examples typical of the kind of experimentation and research that any speaker can conduct to gather material. Use your imagination in preparing your speeches so that you can produce this lively kind of evidence. Be careful that the facts gleaned are not pure coincidence and that anyone else would get the same results when performing the same experiment. As you continue to give speeches, the material gained from your own experiments and research will constitute greater and greater proportions of your supporting evidence. People in the field of business and industry are in a position to conduct this experimentation or have it done within their own institution. Observation of the results furnishes the greater part of the material they use in their speeches.

Using the Library

Inevitably, the library will constitute one of the most important sources of material, but it should be approached in an organized way to further your analysis and gather support material and to save time and energy. Browsing in the library is always interesting and as a student you should do as much as possible, but in a busy world you will frequently not have the time.

Have a Research Plan

The great speech educator Kim Giffin once told his class in research methods, "If you aim at nothing you will surely hit it." When gathering materials to build arguments, you must confront the modern library and the huge gateway to information it represents with a plan. That plan should not be narrowly focused on just the one or two facts or opinions that you are seeking, but should take into account that your argumentation will be superior if it is built on all sides of the issue; in addition, you should know what you don't know and take into account useful information that you will come across during your research.

Know What You Want to Find Out. Too often students depend on the library to provide them with all the information they need. As you are now aware, you can gather information from a wide variety of other sources. By the time you go to the library, you should have already constructed a list of possible arguments. You can then use the library to find information that supports or refutes them.

Develop Search Terms. You will use search terms to find the specific information you need in the library. An effective search term is both inclusive and exclusive: It will include everything you are looking for while excluding anything irrelevant. The subject terms from the Library of Congress work well for this purpose. You can find them at http://www.loc.gov/search/. Terms used in your topic area can also be good search terms. For example, critical pedagogy is a specific term used in education literature to reflect a rather specific school of thought.

Authors who write extensively on your topic can also make good search terms. Using their names as search terms will also yield some decent results, though certainly not all that is written on your topic.

Add Additional Goals and Key Words as Your Search Progresses. The library research process is a good model of the general learning process. At each point in the process you gain new information that you subsequently use and take advantage of. You should try to keep a running list of search words and terms that work well for you and also authors that seem dominant in the field. New search term variations will lead you to new arguments as well as new forms of support for arguments you have already discovered.

Utilize Library Resources

Most libraries understand that new users need help. If you feel you need assistance, ask at the front desk upon entering. This can be useful even if you are an experienced researcher in a new library, as you can get a map of the library showing the location of its various holdings. Remember that libraries are increasingly designed to be "gateways" for people to get the information they need as opposed to stuffy and overly academic institutions used only by scholars and advanced students.

Most major libraries make the following kinds of materials available. Some libraries will have more and some will have less, but a look into these holdings should provide a fairly comprehensive start to your research effort.

Reference Materials. Most libraries have a reference section, often with a reference desk and reference librarian, where materials that are primarily factually informative are located. A reference librarian can be of immense value to you not only in finding reference materials but also in guiding you to other library resources.

Useful holdings in the reference section of most libraries include:

+ Dictionaries: general dictionaries and specialized dictionaries focusing on one field, such as legal dictionaries;

+ Almanacs: various statistical compilations with either a general or a specific focus;

+ Encyclopedias: multivolume general encyclopedias containing information in alphabetical order by topic, or smaller, more specialized encyclopedias such as the *Encyclopedia of Philosophy;*

+ Biographical information: general and specific lists of persons in various fields;

+ Atlases: compendiums of geographical and topographical maps and information;

+ Short histories: specialized volumes that discuss the historical progress of a variety of locations or disciplines;

+ Indexes: listings of where other materials can be found, for example, *Reader's Guide to Periodical Literature, Social Science Index, Citation Abstract*, and others;

+ Other resources: many reference departments have local and national telephone books, local directories, and other sources of factual materials.

Although the reference section of the library can provide you with useful information, much of it tends to be background information that can then guide you in searching for additional materials. If you lack a basic background in a subject, such as a specific country or school of philosophy, the reference section is an excellent first stop in your research effort that will be further refined by what you find there.

Online Resources. Many libraries have an assortment of electronic resources. The reference librarian can describe the holdings and offer you advice on the best materials to use. These are often resources that libraries pay for so they may not be available from computer stations outside of the library. Some of the most useful resources include:

- Congressional Quarterly Researcher, http://library2.cqpress.com/cqresearcher/;
- EBSCO Research, http://support.epnet.com/CustSupport/AboutUs/AboutUs.asp;
- EHRAF Collections of Ethnography, http://library2.cqpress.com/cqresearcher/;
- Global Books in Print, http://www.globalbooksinprint.com/Global-BooksInPrint/;
- InfoTrac Databases, http://web5.infotrac.galegroup.com/itw/infomark/;
- JSTOR journal storage, http://www.jstor.org/demo.shtml;
- Lexis-Nexis databases, http://www.lexis-nexis.com/;
- Project Muse scholarly journals online, http://muse.jhu.edu/about/contact.html.

For current events and legal research, the Lexis-Nexis databases are the most useful. They contain full-text articles from a huge selection of magazines, newspapers, wire services, medical journals, and law journals. The search functions are easy to use and powerful. You can find articles on specific subjects through a title search and can also do a full-text search to find any mention of your subject in millions of different articles. These will often yield hundreds and hundreds of specific articles, so use the power search function and limit your search by key words, type of search (newspapers, magazines, law journals), and date.

Periodicals. Periodicals can be a valuable source of current and specific information about a controversial issue. Many of these publications specialize in specific subjects and may also represent specific perspectives on topics, such as a political magazine that tends to emphasize one area of the ideological spectrum. The electronic resources discussed above will not be comprehensive when looking for materials in periodicals, so avoid the temptation to utilize only the electronic resources because they are a bit easier to use.

You can find articles in magazines and periodicals by using the guides found in the reference section, such as the *Reader's Guide to Periodical Literature*. However, because not all libraries can afford to carry all magazines and journals, you will need to determine if your library has what you are looking for. Most libraries have a list of their periodical holdings, which will also assist you in finding publications that you may have missed in your other searches. Many research libraries have a periodicals section and a periodicals librarian who can help you.

Past issues of periodicals are often bound together and stored on shelves, arranged alphabetically by the title of the publication. You can find recent issues in a current periodicals area where they are located unbound on shelves, also arranged alphabetically by title. The authors have found it useful to locate periodical titles that might be specific to a given research topic and browse through the tables of contents of the most recent issues, as often they have not yet been fully indexed. Unfortunately, some periodicals will not be available because they are being bound in their transition from the current periodicals shelves to the bound periodicals shelves.

Books. The vast majority of libraries have now replaced their card catalogue indexes of books with electronic indexes that are much easier to search and browse through. Usually a number of computer terminals will be available in the library for this purpose. You can search by author or title but to research a topic, searching by subject key word is usually more useful. This kind of search often will yield a long list of books that you can evaluate before seeking out the physical volumes. One way to narrow your list is by looking at the publication date. For controversial issues, you will want to consult the most recent books. Quite often the full titles of the volumes will also help you make your determination.

When you have determined the books you want to consider, find their call numbers (the code used to find them on the shelves where books are located). Then organize your list by call number so you can find the volumes easily. Scan the titles on the shelves around the books that you do find, you might make some serendipitous discoveries.

Do not be discouraged if you locate a larger number of books than you wish to read. You do not have to read an entire book when in the process of argumentative research. The index or the table of contents will help you locate the specific information you need. When you find useful material, pay attention to citations and footnotes as these will lead you to other books and articles on your subject.

Inter-Library Loan. Always begin your research early so that you have time to digest and evaluate materials you find. An early start will also allow you to gain access to materials not in your library by using inter-library loan. Consult a librarian or an inter-library loan office about the specific procedures. Some libraries limit this privilege to certain categories of users or may limit the number of requests you can make. These requests can take days or weeks, so be patient. You must also use these materials quickly; your library will have to return them to the library of origin within a short time.

United States Government Documents. Many research libraries are also depositories for United States government documents. Although many of these documents are now available electronically through the "Thomas" website (http://www.thomas.gov), much of value is still to be found in hard copies of such government documents because they can be read without needing a computer. The Government Printing Office also produces a *Catalog of U.S. Government Publications.*

Following is a list of the types of government documents that are most useful for argumentative researchers:

- *Congressional Record:* transcripts of sessions in the Senate and House of Representatives.

- Congressional hearings: investigative and informative sessions held by the committees of the two houses of Congress to examine specific issues, programs, and proposals. These are particularly useful for argumentative researchers because all sides of a given issue are usually represented, with many expert witnesses being called to testify.

- Department publications: various departments of the executive branch will publish documents about their programs and procedures.

- Government research agencies: these agencies have been established to investigate and research government activities as well as social needs. The Government Accounting Office (GAO) is a "watchdog" agency that publishes a large number of reports on existing programs and the needs of the society. Similarly, the Congressional Budget Office (CBO) publishes reports on a wide variety of subjects, often with a focus on budgetary and appropriations issues. Each department also has a watchdog or inspector general's office that publishes useful documents.

Multimedia. More and more libraries are expanding their multimedia holdings. These include audiotapes, videotapes, DVDs, and videodiscs of documentaries and historic film footage that may be useful in understanding your issue. Some libraries have viewing or listening stations so that you can use these materials in the library while others allow these materials to circulate. Many libraries include multimedia items in their general catalogues; others maintain a separate listing. Consult a librarian to determine the specific procedures for accessing them.

Consult a Librarian for Additional Assistance. If you have questions during your library visit, consult the librarians. You should not feel that you are inconveniencing them or that you are showing your ignorance about how to use a library. Librarians not only know their collections but are also experts in finding information and are there to assist you. A wise researcher considers them a valuable resource.

INTERNET RESEARCH

People tend to use the Internet extensively to gather information and evidence. Many believe that students rely too heavily on the Internet to gather information and neglect other excellent sources of information. Do not fall victim to the allure of simply sitting in front of a computer screen to gather all the information you need.

The most important fact to remember about information gathered from the Internet is that it is not generally reviewed and screened. Any unqualified person can put views or information on a web page. Books and newspapers have editors, and they still contain substantial amounts of less-than-credible information, so imagine how much more misinformation is posted on unreviewed Internet sites. Find out who has written the information you are gathering and apply the tests of authority mentioned earlier. The Internet contains a huge amount of excellent information, but you must still examine the source critically.

Most Internet users locate the information they want through the use of Internet search engines—sites where you can type in your subject and receive a list of possible web pages to view. These search engine sites come and go with some regularity. One good resource for finding search engines and comparing them is Search Engine Watch at http://searchenginewatch.com/links/.

Some major search engines to consider:

+ Google: http://www.google.com is the most preferred search engine site, voted four times best search engine by Search Engine Watch readers.

+ Yahoo: http://www.yahoo.com is very useful because of its extensive directory system that allows you to find related sites that your keyword search may have missed.

+ Ask Jeeves: http://www.ask.com allows you to ask questions in natural language and often finds the answer you seek very quickly.

Search engines for global topics can be found at:

http://searchenginewatch.com/links/article.php/2156281/.

Search engines that are operated by volunteers and members of specific communities can be found at:

http://searchenginewatch.com/links/article.php/2156101/.

Try to limit the number of irrelevant results you receive by utilizing the advanced features of many of these search engines. In addition, when looking at resulting references, do so with a very critical eye.

In recording the source of information you find on the Internet, use the standards provided for print information but also make sure to include the URL (universal resource locator or web address), determine which individual or group is the author of the content, and also the date when you viewed the page, as often web pages change quickly or disappear altogether.

Recording Your Data

As you gather your material, keep your goal—its use to influence belief—in mind. Accuracy in quotations and factual data is essential. Therefore, you must record your research in such a way that it may be utilized easily on the speaking platform. Here are some suggestions of the more commonly used methods:

1. Use word processing pages or sheets of paper of uniform size; use separate pages for separate bits of information. Pages can be printed out for use in an oral argument or can be read from the screen of a laptop.

2. Develop a method of filing these papers; consider buying a small file box such as most bookstores carry.

3. Place only one fact or opinion on a sheet. This is essential if you wish to file the sheets in the proper order.

4. Place at the top of the sheet the main issue (the name of the argument that the recorded evidence supports) or subordinate issue to which the material refers.

5. At either the top or the bottom of the sheet, write the name of the person who gathered the facts or uttered opinions. We have already discussed the importance of sources in gaining audience belief.

6. Either at the top or bottom of the sheet, indicate the title of the person you are quoting or using as an authority. This usually would be the title of the most important position she holds. Often you will keep separate sheets of biographical information about people from whom you gathered your data. On these sheets you should dedicate a space to record that source's various qualifications and other information that adds to the credibility of the source.

7. At the top or bottom of the sheet indicate the exact source of your information. If it is a publication, give the name of the book or pamphlet, the date of publication, and the page from which it was copied. This is important because you may want to reread the material and will want to know where you can find it in a hurry. This is particularly important should a dispute arise over your factual data and others wish to check your information. If the source was a magazine, write down the name, the date of publication, and the page, and usually the volume number. If the material was derived from any of the other sources, indicate the source of the material—a personal interview, a letter written on a certain date, an original experiment, etc. If you are using an Internet source, make sure to include the URL (universal resource locator, or web address) and the date when you viewed it.

8. The main body of the sheet will consist chiefly of direct quotations. If you summarize a longer paragraph in your own words, use parentheses.

9. Avoid long quotations and let most of your recorded data be facts rather than opinions, as factual data almost always are more powerful than opinions in influencing conduct. At the same time, don't forget that opinions of authorities add psychological weight to your arguments.

Wherever possible, however, let the stated opinion of your authority be brief. Long quotations tend to become tedious for your audience.

10. Write on only one side of the sheet. This will expedite its use as you speak.

11. Assemble your data in your file box on the basis of the subject heading of each sheet. If a particular sheet has data that might support more than one argument, make additional copies so that a separate sheet can be filed under each argument that the data might support.

Data so recorded will be easy to use when you are speaking. Many speakers use the method of outlining the development of a particular argument on one sheet and then clipping to it the support material sheets, so they have the outline of a particular argument in front of them. As they need factual data, they pull out the first sheet containing support material and read it to the audience. They can then proceed to the second and third and fourth sheets as needed. Furthermore, if they are in a committee session or a discussion program, they will have additional material available to strengthen their particular argument when they are questioned or need reinforcement. Following are examples of the two methods of recording data on your sheet:

Topic: Each State That Obtains Nuclear Weapons Increases Risk of Cataclysm

Andrew Goodpaster, steering committee on eliminating weapons of mass destruction, Henry Stimson Center 1997, *The Washington Quarterly*, Summer. "The Declining Utility of Nuclear Weapons," pg. 92

"Most importantly, the very existence of nuclear weapons entails a risk that these weapons will be used one day, with devastating consequences for the United States and other nations. The manipulation of nuclear risk in U.S.-Soviet relations, as during the Cuban Missile Crisis and the 1973 Middle Eastern crisis, by its nature implied a danger that a crisis could escalate and end in a cataclysmic nuclear exchange. In the multipolar structure of international relations chat characterizes the post–Cold War period, the risks of nuclear use could increase with every new nuclear power."

In this chapter we have tried to suggest the best methods of gathering material that will influence others. We have suggested that you can increase your motivation for getting material by remembering that the material becomes the information for changing the opinion of others. Second, we have suggested places to look for your material. Before you go to the library, consider your own knowledge and thinking, using an organized method of listing the arguments and facts that you already know. Exchange opinions and knowledge with others, gather vivid material of direct experience by observing the thing in operation, and conduct your own original experimentation and research. Then augment all these by using the library and the Internet in an organized fashion. Last, remembering that you will want to make use of the material gathered in your speech, develop good habits of note taking that will make the material readily available while speaking.

1. Define:

   a. Gathering material

   b. Research

   c. Support material

2. Students often speak of writing a "research" paper. Explain why they are misusing the term research in its strictest meaning.

3. What should be your motivation for gathering material?

4. Why should you develop an organized system for gathering material?

5. List the five general sources from which you can gather material.

6. In gathering material from your own knowledge and thinking, what are the five lists that you will make?

7. In exchanging opinions and knowledge with others, what are the three sources of information?

8. Why should you ask only for specific information in a letter or e-mail?

9. Why is direct observation such a valuable source of material?

10. Why is conducting original experimentation or research valuable when the results can already be found in publications?

11. Select two propositions on which you might speak and indicate some original research that you might conduct to support your arguments.

12. The authors give an organized plan for the use of the library. What is it?

13. Indicate specifically the steps you would take in finding the following material:

   a. You are given the task of introducing a prominent admiral to an audience and wish to discover various facts in her life that you might wish to utilize in the introduction.

   b. You wish to find the profits of the European Union steel industry for 2004.

   c. You wish to find the number of AIDS cases in the United States in the past five years.

   d. You wish to gather information about terrorist incidents that have occurred in the past two years.

e. You would like a good definition of the law of supply and demand.

f. You wish to discover the most pressing current problems confronting your local city government.

g. You wish to discover the more frequently used arguments, pro and con, on abolishing capital punishment.

h. You would like to get a brief history of the major demonstrations that occurred in Lebanon during the last year.

i. You need information in order to give a brief history of intercollegiate debating in the United States.

j. You wish to make an intensive study of Internet-related legislation and want to begin with specific studies in the field.

k. You wish to gather proof that crime has been decreasing in the United States during the past few years.

l. You would like to know the Rose Bowl champion for 1954.

m. You would like to know the average personal income for various occupational groups in the United States.

14. Make out two evidence sheets that will support the particular argument. Let one be a sheet on which you have statistical data and let the second be an opinion of an authority. See to it that the two sheets demonstrate all the principles involved in recording data.

Chapter 5
Influencing Through Evidence

Not long ago a local businesswoman came to us quite discouraged because too many people in her estimation believed that businesspeople were greedy. She said, "I have become so disturbed about this that I have been giving a speech on this subject to various audiences, as well as talking about it to everybody I can, but somehow I can't get them to agree. I wonder why?" She happened to have a copy of her speech written out and we went over it together. After reading the speech, it was quite obvious why she hadn't changed attitudes. She just didn't have the information for changing belief. This information is evidence. She had many arguments, but she had failed to support them with facts. Thus, she was presenting a speech that consisted merely of the expression of her own opinions and ideas about businesspeople in general, opinions that they were not charging too high prices, opinions that they were not greedy. She needed evidence. You, too, will need evidence if you are to get others to agree with you. Let us consider how to influence others through the use of evidence.

DEFINITION OF EVIDENCE

Evidence is any matter of fact used in gaining the belief or changing attitudes of others. It is any factual matter used to prove a proposition. Reasoning is a process of drawing conclusions from facts or truths. We often call the conclusion drawn by this process "inference." When an inference is drawn from facts or truths and used to gain belief or change attitudes, we have the process of argument. Thus, evidence is a dominant element of argument. A distinction may be made between the use of evidence for argument and the use of facts in general study. Argument is a process of communication, a process of gaining the belief of other people, and facts are necessary to it. In general study and in discussion where we are not trying to change attitudes, facts are used to substantiate conclusions. Here the process is one of reasoning from facts to conclusions. The advocate, then, uses the same process as we do in general study but demonstrates her process to an audience or to listeners in an attempt to influence them.

Types of Evidence

Evidence comes in various kinds and different forms; below is a discussion of them.

Factual Examples

A factual example is evidence because it was an actual occurrence. It did happen and was witnessed. An auto accident happens. The witnesses either observe it or the damaged automobile reveals it. The narration of the true events of the accident constitutes fact. In using the example of the automobile accident to support an argument, you may narrate the story at length. In this case, the name often applied is "illustration." Often examples are merely alluded to. We say, for instance, that there were three accidents yesterday, one on Main Street, another on Maple Street, and another on College Street. These now constitute examples that could be used to support an argument. We should make sure that we know the difference between a factual and a hypothetical example. A hypothetical example is one that might have happened. Often we will use hypothetical examples in exposition. Hypothetical examples may be used to explain an argument but they do not constitute evidence to support it. You make a stronger argument when you use either the long or short factual example, even while explaining, rather than the hypothetical. A factual example will influence belief while the hypothetical may not.

Statistics

Statistics are but a compilation of factual examples. Statistics used to support arguments appear most frequently in terms of total number of cases, percentage of cases, or ratio of cases (e.g., one out of every four). Less frequently they appear in the form of index figures, critical ratios, or correlations. Sometimes they will be presented in graphic form. Statistics constitute evidence because they are a summary of things that did occur. *Percentages, index figures, critical ratios,* and *correlations* are merely mathematical terms used to indicate the frequency of occurrence.

Opinions of Authorities

Authorities in any field are individuals who are trained in research, have made studies, are free from prejudice and exaggeration, and are consistent. Opinions of authorities constitute evidence in that the opinions are supposed to be based on the research they have done. Presumably they have studied great numbers of cases, have had long experience in observing, and, as a result, have arrived at conclusions based on these studies and experience. Audiences will accept such persons as authorities if they live up to these tests and particularly if the audience already recognizes them as authorities. Sometimes the best evidence to support a given argument is the testimony of those who are considered authorities on the question involved. In court trials, the testimony of psychiatrists about the sanity of the defendant is the best means of gaining belief. Often, the opinions of persons who have studied the subject for a long time are utilized; in some propositions this is about the only type of evidence you have, particularly in many phases of our international relations and the development of our foreign policy.

Testimony of Lay Witnesses

Often individuals are called on to testify about the events of an occurrence in question. These witnesses are untrained observers and are called "lay witnesses." Although they are untrained observers, what they report can be taken as factual. As long as they report their own observations and not their inferences, their testimony is factual in nature. Court trials make great use of lay witnesses, whose testimony is used in determining guilt or innocence. Public opinion polls are but the gathering of the testimony of average citizens.

Documents, Legal Papers, and the Like

Many kinds of documents and legal papers, utilized as proof, constitute evidence. A birth certificate is accepted as valid proof of either age or nationality. A marriage license affords proof that a marriage has occurred. Deeds plus their recording by town or county clerks constitute proof of ownership of land. Still another document to be offered as proof of ownership is a bill of sale. All these and many others may be used as special forms of proof on certain occasions. Documents and legal papers, then, frequently constitute proof on special occasions and less frequently on general speaking occasions. Their most frequent use is in court procedures.

The foregoing are the five kinds of evidence available to the speaker. The last two have the greatest use in court trials. You will make use of the first three much more often on general speaking occasions. In the rest of this chapter we will concern ourselves with arguments to validate or invalidate evidence. Inasmuch as we are concerned with the task of the general use of argument rather than the more specific application in the courtroom, we shall concern ourselves with the first three rather than the last two. Should you need to make use of the last two types in courtroom procedures, the special rules set forth by your own state or the federal government will supply you with tests for accuracy and how they may or may not be used.

ARGUMENTS TO VALIDATE EVIDENCE FROM AUTHORITIES

As we have indicated, authorities (individuals who have made a prolonged study of a subject) are used in two different ways in presenting evidence for argument. You will quote their opinions and you will offer factual examples or statistics that they have gathered. Authorities should have been specially trained and should have actually gathered original data in the field. Many of the people quoted as authorities in a particular field are not. To gain the belief of an audience, you need lines of argument to increase the prestige of your authority. The following are the ones that you will use most frequently.

The Authority Has Made a Study

If you can reveal to your audience that the individual whose opinions you are quoting or who has reported statistics or examples has spent a great deal of time making a study of the subject, you increase the value of your argument. For example, you can strengthen belief in reports that Americans have too much credit card debt by showing that your source conducted a detailed national study of it over a three-year period. Her material did not come from the library, but from original sources. The researcher did the observing herself. The chemist in the laboratory who has spent years discovering a new formula has learned much from that experience and has become an authority in the area in which he has worked. Consider another example: Scientists have developed a vaccine against meningitis. Many individuals were involved in developing the vaccine. After it was developed, researchers tested it in various cities. Using what are known as experimental methods, investigators gave the vaccine to large number of individuals and then matched the people treated with others who were not so treated. The experiment was conducted over a period of time and proved that the population treated with the vaccine had a lower rate of meningitis than the population that was not. The report of the study's findings becomes a good source to quote on the subject of meningitis vaccine. To quote such an authority to support your argument strengthens it; to reveal to your audience that the individual quoted has given a great deal of time to actual experimentation and study validates the facts that you are using.

The Authority Was Trained in Research

This line of argument strengthens the validity of your facts on the grounds that to conduct original research, an individual must be trained. She must be trained to observe impartially; she must be trained to know all the fallacies or pitfalls in gathering data. To illustrate—many organizations and institutions throughout our country have as their chief reasons for being the gathering of information and the conducting of original research. They hire large staffs of trained people. That training consists of a good education and probably includes a doctorate, which requires training in research. Furthermore, to be hired for such a job, the individual should have had some experience in performing outside research. Through training and experience such persons become qualified to gather the information that you and I read in statistical tables. Statistical tables are, therefore, as reliable as those who compile them. You can rest assured that data developed by qualified organizations are probably highly reliable.

National governments have many bureaus that gather factual data. The U.S. Department of Commerce, which publishes a survey of current business, has qualified people to compile the data. Private institutions such as the Brookings Institute hire only experienced researchers. Presidents of the United States are often quoted as authorities on certain subjects. Certainly they are authorities on various aspects of their job as president, but when they use statistics, the probabilities are great that they did not make the study and compile the figures nor are they necessarily trained in research.

The Authority Is Free from Prejudice

You will increase the weight of your evidence if you demonstrate that the authority quoted is an impartial observer, or that, if he is prejudiced, the probabilities are that he is prejudiced in the direction opposite the facts cited. People engaged in a cause, environmental activists or spokespeople for industry, for example, are likely to report factual data or express the opinions favoring one side of a dispute because they are fighting for that cause. College professors are often quoted as authorities not only because they are trained in research in their subject, but also because they have no stake in one side or another of public controversy. They can, as it were, "sit by the side of the road" and watch the controversy without becoming emotionally involved. At least they are in a position to be more impartial than a person who is in the middle of the struggle, someone whose very livelihood or prestige depends on winning the battle for her side. Many organizations are engaged in a cause. Part of their work is to publish factual data, but often the facts reported give an incomplete picture because they are slanted in the direction of the aims of the organization.

The Authority Is Free from Exaggeration

This line of argument will strengthen your evidence on the grounds that it is accurate rather than overdrawn or one-sided. Many times you read speeches or editorials and wish to quote from them. The speaker or editorial writer may be guilty of exaggeration because he has selected only the worst cases or the extremes rather than the average. Exaggeration leaves the impression that the extreme is normal or typical. I remember a speaker talking on great differences in income. She was quite effective because she cited only the highest of incomes and the lowest, but an exaggeration of the true picture resulted. Another speaker was always adding a little bit to the statistics he quoted. He always wanted them to sound a little stronger and so he rounded them up, making them larger. Such techniques should be avoided by the responsible advocate.

The Authority Is Consistent

This line of argument strengthens the value of your evidence because it reveals to your audience that the studies or facts given by the authority at various times in her life are not contradictory. A statement made at one time can be reconciled with statements made at another time. This line of argument is frequently necessary when the authority quoted has changed his opinion under changing conditions. For example, Senator John Kerry voting in favor of the invasion of Iraq in 2003 after having voted against the Persian Gulf War of 1990–91 seemed inconsistent. How can this be reconciled? Simply by noting that the greater consistency of the person lay in the principle of the ability to keep the mind open and change opinion as changing conditions and new facts demanded. An authority may advocate a certain economic program on the grounds that it will raise wages and lower prices. On the face of it, this seems inconsistent. But if she proceeds to dig deeply enough to show how much prices can be lowered and how much wages can be raised as a result of the program and thus reconcile the difference, she is not inconsistent. To be able to reveal this to your audience makes the evidence more credible.

These five lines of argument are available to you to strengthen the credibility of the authority whose opinion you quote or whose facts you use. These lines are essential in a free discussion occurring in a debate or discussion or committee meeting when the majority of your audience believes the opposite of your argument. If you can establish your authorities in this way, your audience may very well be won over, in any case, they will find it difficult to believe anything to the contrary.

ARGUMENTS TO INVALIDATE OR REFUTE EVIDENCE FROM AUTHORITIES

These lines of argument are exactly opposite to the five above. In each case we merely substitute a negative term. However, let us investigate more carefully just how you will use such arguments.

The Authority Quoted Did Not Make a Study

You may use this line of argument in this way. "A famous baseball star announces that he uses a particular popular prescription tablet to enhance male sexual performance. We would like to know if he made a study of this drug. Has he gone out into the field and done research about men using this drug? Has he taken the time from his baseball playing and from his training regimen to gather any additional data? Consider another example used in a debate on universal health care.

> The gentleperson quoted Ms. Y as saying that 100,000 people die annually of diseases that could be prevented if we had a better system of paying for medical care. We question whether Ms. Y has had the time to take from her job as Secretary of the Health and Human Services to have made an original study of the issue. It is doubtful that she has, and one considers that to make this statement she should have made a study in which she conducted original experimentation. She would have to take a

group of individuals operating under a private system of payment and note the number of persons that died of various diseases. Then she would have to match them with an equal number of individuals who were living in a country that had universal health care, have kept records of their diseases, and have found that fewer died under that system. Such a study would take a great deal of time. We doubt if such a study has ever been made. Until the gentleperson can reveal that Ms. Y has made such a study and has found such results, her argument is hardly worthy of your belief.

Sitting in as judges for this particular debate, we were quite duly impressed with the foregoing argument to invalidate the opinion of Ms. Y, concluding that Ms. Y's opinion was largely political rhetoric as opposed to hard data. We suggest that you develop your ability to use this line of argument in a similar fashion.

The Authority Quoted Was Not Trained in Research

To use this line of argument you will indicate how the supposed authority lacked the training or experience necessary to qualify her to make a statistical study or express such an opinion. For example:

They tell us that Miss Jones, the great movie star, says, "Maximum Effects facial cleanser is the best for a good complexion." Is Miss Jones a good research chemist? Has she been so well trained in chemistry and dermatology that she can go into a laboratory, apply all the different soaps on the market to live human subjects, observe the effects on human skin, and then report the impartial testimony that one soap is better than all others? We suspect that Miss Jones has been far too busy as an actress to become a research chemist or a dermatologist.

The technique of this argument is to set up the criteria of training and experience necessary for a good authority in the field and reveal how far short the individual falls from being qualified to conduct research in that subject. This argument is effective against individuals who speak on subjects foreign to their background or training and experience. The world's leaders and other high officials often have to speak on subjects about which they have had little experience or training. The line of argument that "the alleged authority was not trained in that field" will aid in invalidating any argument built on such evidence.

The Authority Quoted Is Prejudiced

To use this argument, reveal to your audience the personal stake the authority has in making the statement or reporting the particular example or statistic. Ballplayers, actors, and other prominent individuals are paid to endorse products. The objectives of labor union leaders is to get the highest wages, the best working conditions, the legislation most favorable to their members; they have other objectives but these are basic. Likewise, despite other good objectives and services, the National Association of Manufacturers, the Chamber of Commerce, the Farm Bureau, agricultural cooperatives, and other professional and occupational organizations have as their basic goal the promotion of the interests of their members. Officials and members of such organizations will be expressing opinions, reporting examples and statistics favorable to their particular causes. You can aid the invalidation of arguments built on such evidence if you can reveal that "he was paid to say that," or that "her prejudice would lead her to select those particular examples or statistics favorable to her cause," or that "his prestige and success in his chosen field demands that he say that."

The Authority Quoted Is Guilty of Exaggeration

To use this line of argument effectively you should be able to reveal to your audience either that the authority consistently selects only the worst cases or that he has a habit of implying that the extreme cases are the average. In a debate on the legalization of gambling, this following line of argument was rather effectively used:

> The speaker has quoted an authority saying that there are many Mafia members within legalized gambling enterprises. We would suggest that both the authority and the speaker are guilty of gross exaggeration. Even our congressional committees in investigating the number of mafia members among the hundreds upon hundreds of legal gambling operators could only find fewer than 100 and chiefly were able to uncover mafia activity of any degree among less than twenty individuals. Anyone who would lead you to believe that mafia involvement in legalized gambling is typical is guilty of gross exaggeration.

To use this line of argument effectively you will need to know the statistics germane to the proposition at hand. Be mindful that many authorities quoted in a given field are energetic in making the case for reform as strong as possible. They emphasize the bad things and unwittingly leave the impression that the worst is typical. Study the statistics of incidence of the problem to use this line of argument effectively.

The Authority Quoted Is Guilty of Inconsistency

This line of argument will probably be used much less frequently than the preceding four. Persons who are logical and who have integrity tend to be consistent in their behavior. Furthermore, many seeming inconsistencies are not inconsistent, but are frequently the result of inadequacies in language. For example, those who say they dislike big government but advocate increased local government activity. A refinement of language soon reveals that they oppose big government at the national level and would limit it by strengthening local government.

On the other hand, some individuals are definitely inconsistent because they are swayed by popular opinion. Politicians, caught between trying to vote as they think their constituencies would like and their own thinking, are often inconsistent. The story is told of the representative who gave a speech in Congress one day on one side of the subject and then the following day gave a speech on the opposite side. When told that a person of principle would hardly be so inconsistent, the congressman replied, "Sometimes a person must rise above principle." Obviously, he had heard from his constituents back home. Even the best of us fall into inconsistencies when applying principles from one case to another. These should then be pointed out in an argument. What is the technique? Take the statement of an authority on one case and then a statement made at a later time and show that they are diametrically opposed. The following is an example of its use: "The gentleperson a few weeks ago in speaking of the refugees from Sudan said that we should be more lenient in our immigration laws in order to open our doors to those downtrodden individuals. Yet today she takes the exact opposite stand with reference to refugees from Asia. She is hardly consistent in her thinking."

ARGUMENTS TO VALIDATE AND INVALIDATE STATISTICS

Statistics, when they are properly used and properly validated, become some of the strongest resources for persuasion. On the other hand, when misused by charlatans to mislead audiences, they become a thing of evil. A good student of argument thoroughly studies their use and becomes effective in their presentation on the platform. Many have maligned statistics, and many find them dull. On the other hand, a speaker who is effective in their use may find them not only strong in supporting arguments but effective in arousing the emotions of audiences as well. When a speaker knows how to interpret them and use them to stir the imagination of the listener, statistics become particularly effective. Following are four of the most commonly used lines of argument to validate or invalidate statistics.

Has the Unit of the Statistics Been Carefully Defined?

If you are going to use statistics to influence audiences effectively, you must be sure that the audience has a clear picture of the units within your statistics. To suggest that a particular bureau has been successful in 98 percent of its cases is rather meaningless unless the speaker defines "success." To use statistics effectively, you must often precede them by careful definition and often by even greater elaboration that makes use of either the factual example or the longer factual illustration. The line of argument "that the speaker has failed to define her unit of statistics" is extremely effective to completely invalidate the statistical bedrock of another's argument. Consider the following use of this line of argument:

> The gentleperson tells us that the victims of illegal toxic waste disposal have failed to win 98 percent of their lawsuits. She fails to define for us what she means by the word "win." If "win" means only that they have failed to win a formal court judgment, this may ignore the fact that the companies have engaged in large out-of-court settlements in the vast majority of cases to avoid harmful publicity Until the gentleperson can define for us exactly what she means by "win" and show that the defendant companies have not settled out-of-court, we can hardly agree with her at this point; we can hardly believe that the harms of illegal toxic waste dumping were not very real even if not pursued to final judgment . . .

In using this line of argument to evaluate or refute, the debater sets up a criterion of definition and then reveals how far short his opponent has fallen in fulfilling it. In the foregoing example, you would set up realistic criteria for the measurement of the harms of illegal toxic waste disposal.

Are the Statistical Units an Accurate Index of What We Want to Know?

Statistics become an accurate index only when they reveal exactly what is needed to support the argument. The number of students making unauthorized notes for an exam is hardly an accurate index to dishonesty. Some of those students make such notes only to throw them away; at the same time, many other ways are available to cheat on an exam. The use of such notes during the exam is a problem, not the making of them. In the same fashion, a rising cost of living is hardly an index to the difficulties that people may have in paying their bills; their income may be rising even more rapidly than the cost of living. Similarly, an increase in the number of crimes is not an index to increasing rates of crime if population is growing more rapidly than the number of crimes. The more accurate index here is the crime rate per 100, or per 1,000, or per 10,000 people.

The advocate making use of statistics should not only make sure that her statistics are an accurate index of what is wanted but also point out to the audience that she is using the most accurate index. Speakers pointing to the prosperity of a country often use an index showing how real wages have gone up rather than an index of the amount earned per year. Most audiences are quite aware that the dollars of the early years of the twenty first century are worth much less than the dollars of the 1960s. When using statistics, particularly those that are the most significant for gaining belief in your argument, you must show that the statistics you offer are an accurate index to what we want to know.

The line of argument that "the statistics are not an index to what we want to know" is very effective to invalidate or refute statistics. If this charge is well supported, the whole argument may be undermined. Consider the following: "The standard of living of web site designers must be distinctly higher than that of auto workers. The Bureau of Labor Statistics data reveal that web site designers receive, on the average, $10 an hour more for their work." Such an argument can be invalidated as follows:

> The gentleperson would have us believe that just because web site designers get $10 an hour more than auto workers, they have a higher standard of living. She fails to tell us that web site design is not a guaranteed weekly 40-hour job. Since it is irregular, the only significant unit of measurement is annual income. Until the gentleperson can reveal that the annual income of the web site designers is higher than that of factory workers, her argument is unworthy of our belief.

The technique here is one in which: (1) we become aware that the index offered is not a sound one and (2) we point out to an audience what a sound index would be and that until such a sound index is used the argument is not worthy of belief. Consider another example: "Airline A must be making at least twice as much money as Airline B. It has two times as many scheduled flights." This argument can be challenged in several ways. We can doubt the original authenticity of each statement: Is it true that Airline A does have twice as many scheduled flights? We also may use the line of argument that the number of flights is not an index to "making money." Airline A, with all its flights, may have only short ones while Airline B may have chiefly long ones. Airline A might have a unionized workforce or inefficient aircraft. Furthermore, we must be careful in this argument to define what is meant by "making money." The difference between gross income and net income is great. The only accurate index of gross income is the total amount made in a given period. Net income, on the other hand, is the profit earned by a corporation. The most significant aspect of this example is that the total number of flights scheduled is not an index to either gross or net income. By revealing this to an audience, you have done much to invalidate that argument.

Are the Statistical Units Comparable in Terms of Size and Relevance?

As has been suggested before, statistics constitute either a compilation of a number of factual examples or they are a mathematical interpretation of that compilation. These factual examples should be so sufficiently similar that they can be lumped together into one statistical category. The statistics are hardly comparable if one were to lump together 1 murder with 19 traffic violations. Although they may have some similar features, a flu epidemic that hits one town and an epidemic that is national are vastly different.

On the other hand, a certain distribution of factual examples of many kinds takes the form of the bell-shaped curve. Such a distribution exists in such areas as human intelligence, aptitudes, and personality traits and in many other areas. When it does, we have what is called "a normal curve of distribution" if a sufficient number of specific examples are included. Despite the fact that the extremes are so dissimilar, the normal distribution makes it possible for us to lump them together with meaning. Be careful, however, to note whether a concentration of incidents in a particular area throws this normal curve askew.

As an advocate using such statistics, you may often wish to make them more authentic by pointing out to the audience why the units are comparable. Consider the following example: "The investigative efforts of the Environmental Protection Agency (EPA) are a great success. According to its statistics, of the 2,300 toxic landfill sites investigated last year, only 175 were found to be threats to public health." This argument is a good one only if the inspected sites are comparable. On the other hand, consider the following counterargument: "The statistics used by the gentlepersons suggest that the EPA was overwhelmingly successful. The fact that most toxic landfill sites were not identified as public health risks does not indicate that the EPA was successful. One hundred seventy-five huge toxic waste sites that threaten public health are hardly a sign of success. Additionally, the fact that they are 'claimed' to be safe does not make it so." The technique of the speaker using this line of argument was to reveal how disproportionate these two cases were in comparison to the other sites mentioned. Accordingly, as a speaker you should be alert to statistical units that are lumped together in one category—they may not be of comparable size or relevance, and you should develop the ability to reveal this to audiences lest they be misled.

Do Other Studies of the Same Nature Verify These Facts?

Humankind has learned the value of original research to verify its beliefs. Often several studies have been made in the same field. If studies are made and the research is done properly, and if conditions surrounding the area being studied have not changed in any significant manner, the results of one study should approximate the results of another study. For example, many studies have been done on the effect of a driver-training course on the would-be drivers. The various studies tend to support each other in that those individuals who had driver training seem to have fewer accidents and are less likely to break the traffic laws. A speaker who wishes to strengthen her use of statistics can do so by thoroughly explaining one set in developing the argument. Then she can proceed to reveal the information of additional studies, independently made, that verify the same conclusion. For example, some researchers claimed that they had created a "cold fusion" process that could produce almost limitless energy. This was news all around the world until other scientists were unable to replicate and thus confirm their findings. Just because one small group of experts claims something is true does not necessarily mean it is so.

Similarly this line of argument can be used to refute or invalidate statistics. If two researchers conduct similar studies and their findings disagree, any conclusions that are drawn are surrounded by much uncertainty. For example, a few studies, many financed by the oil and coal industries, indicate that the human production of carbon dioxide from the burning of fossil fuels is not an important contributor to climate change. Surveying the literature, even in a cursory fashion, will make clear that the majority of studies and scientists who conduct them find that use of fossil fuels is an important contributor to climate change. One study can come to a conclusion and can be used as evidence, but reference to a contrary preponderance of evidence can overcome that one study. A speaker in using this line of argument points out how other studies have invalidated previous findings or else added information that considerably modifies them. If you want to refute a statistic and can find at least two or, better yet, three or four studies that say exactly the opposite, it can be nullified.

The foregoing lines of argument, five on source and four on statistics, constitute tests for the reliability of evidence. The moment the evidence fails to live up to one or more of these tests, it becomes unreliable. These nine lines of argument, which you will use most frequently in speeches, should be understood and you should develop skill in their use. You will use lines of argument on lay witnesses, documents, and legal papers less frequently unless you are a lawyer. Law courts have their own rules of evidence and a lawyer needs to know these thoroughly.

Below we outline a few such rules but do not develop them extensively because you will not make wide use of them—with one exception: the application of the tests of ordinary witnesses (lay witnesses) in the reporting of everyday occurrences around you. They constitute good tests that may help separate truth from gossip.

Tests of Ordinary Witnesses

Ordinary or lay witnesses are individuals untrained in observing. The following is a list of the tests of whether the testimony they are giving is reliable. These tests can be used as lines of argument to help support what you are saying or to refute or evaluate the arguments of others.

Did the Witness Have the Opportunity to Observe the Happening Directly?

A reliable witness is one who was there and did see the thing happen. She didn't appear afterward and see the aftereffects and draw conclusions, nor did she hear the story from someone else. This latter is called "hearsay" evidence and will be dealt with later.

Was the Witness Physically Capable of Observing the Happening?

One observes through the various senses: sight, hearing, smell, taste, and touch. If the required sense be deficient, an individual would be considered unreliable should that sense be needed for observation. Thus, a person who is colorblind could not testify about green and red signal lights. A person with a loss of hearing could hardly be expected to justify with any degree of accuracy things that had to do with sound. The individual should be physically capable of accurate observation.

Is the Witness Capable of Accurate Reporting?

A variety of questions might be asked about the mental alertness of the individual testifying. Various psychologists have reported tests revealing the inability of people to observe accurately and report what was observed. Memory plays an important role. Some observers have problems putting into words what they have seen and tend to remember only what they verbalize.

Is the Witness Free from Tendencies to Exaggerate?

Some individuals try to "make a good story," one that is exciting or newsworthy out of something they have observed. They make the occurrence bigger than it really was. Always question whether the individual tends to be reliable and accurate or is prone to exaggerate.

Is the Witness Free from Personal Involvement?

The moment an individual becomes personally involved in an occurrence he may have a strong emotional reaction. Once emotionally upset, he distorts the whole incident. For example, an individual involved in an automobile accident may easily fail to observe accurately.

Does the Testimony of the Witness Constitute an Admission?

An admission occurs when a witness reports an incident or gives an opinion that is contrary to what would ordinarily be expected. When considering using this line of argument, the debater should determine if the witness is a layperson or an expert in the field. For instance, for a politician to say that the citizens in her jurisdiction are paying too little in taxes and that rates need to be increased constitutes a distinct admission as it goes against the politician's self-interest. Thus, if a witness is saying something that is against his best interest, the statement may very well be true.

Can It Pass the "Hearsay" Tests?

Whenever somebody tells us something and we pass this on to a third person, this knowledge becomes hearsay for the third individual as well as ourselves. Much information about a variety of events is reported in this fashion and constitutes what is known as "hearsay evidence." Hearsay evidence is considered relatively unreliable unless it can pass two tests. The first: Is the information such that it may be safely passed from one individual to another with substantial accuracy? The second: Are the channels through which the information passed reliable? Much of what we hear about our neighbors would hardly pass either of these two tests. On the other hand, if the president of the senior class were to report in a class meeting that the dean of students had informed her that the board of trustees of the university had raised tuition for the next year, such information would be readily accepted. Thus, if we wish to validate hearsay evidence, we can do so by pointing out that the information was of such a nature that it could be passed from person to person without any substantial change and that the channels through which it came were reliable. We can also invalidate an argument by showing the contrary is true.

TESTS FOR DOCUMENTS AND LEGAL PAPERS

Documents and other legal papers are usually looked on as being authentic. Birth certificates constitute strong proof of age, while marriage certificates constitute equally strong proof of marriage.

The first question to ask is whether the document is an original or a copy. Copies are subject to error and can be changed.

The second question to ask is what the likelihood is of forgery or alteration of the paper. Is there a motive for doing so or is it easy to do? The stronger the motivation for forgery or alteration and the greater the ease of making such changes, the more doubtful we should be of its authenticity. Many college students know how easily identification cards can be changed to indicate that the owner is of an age to purchase liquor.

A third question to ask is whether the legal document is duplicated elsewhere so that it can be verified. Deeds to the possession of land are recorded in the office of the town or county clerk. In fact, this is a universal legal require-ment to verify legal ownership. Local government offices also record such vital information as birth, death, and marriage. Wills are probated in court and their contents recorded. All these authenticate vital data. The duplication of such legal documents and papers makes certain of their existence and makes difficult alteration or change.

Photographic and electronic images have come into greater and greater use in connection with vital information. We make photocopies of papers and documents, and use them as evidence. Pictures are often used to authenticate such things as the presence of an individual at a certain place, as well as the seriousness of such conditions as starvation, disasters, or damage. Just as legal documents can be altered and forged, photographs can as well.

In this chapter we have been concerned with the power of evidence to influence others. We have discussed its definition, the types of evidence available for use along with the lines of argument to validate or invalidate authorities, statistics, and the testimony of ordinary or lay witnesses, and legal documents and papers. As an ordinary speaker you need to know thoroughly, and develop the greatest possible skill in, those lines of argument that will validate or invalidate authorities and statistics. Should you proceed to a more specialized profession such as law, you will need skill in all these areas. Above all, however, you will need to make extensive use of evidence in influencing belief.

EXERCISES

1. Define:
    a. Evidence
    b. Inference
    c. Factual example
    d. Statistics
    e. Opinions of authorities
    f. An ordinary or lay witness
2. Explain why evidence is necessary to change belief.
3. What role does evidence play in the reasoning process?
4. Explain each of the lines of argument by which you can validate or invalidate authorities.

5. Explain each of the lines of argument by which you can validate or invalidate statistics.

6. Explain and give examples of the application of tests of ordinary witnesses.

7. What are the various means by which you can be sure that documents and legal papers are authentic?

8. Use one or more lines of argument on evidence to evaluate or refute the following:

    a. The chairperson of General Motors says, "What is good for General Motors is good for America."

    b. Mister Y, the baseball star, says, "Crunchies are the best breakfast cereal."

    c. Americans are not getting enough exercise. Each year a higher percentage of the American population can be classified as obese.

    d. Our secretary of homeland security says, "We have adopted the best possible security checks to prevent terrorists from infiltrating our airports."

    e. Miss Jones, the great movie star, says, "Maximum Effects is the best facial cleanser for your complexion."

    f. Parental care of children is becoming more and more lax. The head of the FBI reports, "Juvenile crime is on the increase."

    g. The president of the mine workers says, "The workers of our mines have never gotten their fair share of the fruits of industry."

    h. Ms. N, the great television star, says, "Frescodent toothpaste will give you a sexier smile."

    i. The American Automobile Association reports show that Nevada spends more per capita on roads than New York. Obviously, Nevada must have better roads than New York.

    j. The president of Iran says at the United Nations, "Iran wants only peace with the United States."

    k. The head of the FBI testifies that the chief causes of divorce lie in hasty marriages.

    l. In a study of stutterers, Professor Mildred Berry of Rockford College found more twins in the families of the stutterers than in the families of the nonstutterers used as a control group. Therefore, a relationship must exist between stuttering and twins.

m. The secretary of defense says, "The army is better equipped than it has ever been."

n. We can readily conclude that the people today are having trouble paying for hospital care. The president of the Association of American Hospitals reports, "Due to increased costs, we have had to double our charges on hospital services over the past 10 years."

o. A recent candidate for president of the United States says that Wall Street is doing its best to control this country.

p. Howard Mental Health Services of Vermont reports hundreds of successful mental health interventions each week.

q. Because local education in the United States is financed by property taxes, localities with higher property values will have better educational systems.

Chapter 6
Influencing Through Induction

"An illustration is a window in an argument and lets in light." Thus spoke the great preacher, Henry Ward Beecher, in his Yale Lectures. That advice should be heeded by any student who wishes to become effective in using argument because it furnishes a strong clue to the strength of inductive reasoning in influencing audiences. Whenever a speaker cites one factual example to "let in light," and then follows it with a second and a third, and finally climaxes the argument with overall statistics, she is using one of the most powerful tools for gaining belief.

PROPOSITIONS WITH WHICH INDUCTION IS EFFECTIVE

Induction can be used effectively in gaining the belief of people on propositions of past or present fact or value. Should you, as an advocate, desire to show that "evils exist in the present system," or that "we are confronted with a problem," inductive reasoning will often be a superior method for persuading others. On the other hand, if you choose to defend the present system or policy, induction may be your best weapon; it will permit you to prove that advantage one, advantage two, and so on exist. Almost without exception, the inductive process proves historical trends. Public opinion polls are the result of inductive surveys. The inductive process has verified much of the research in both the sciences and the social sciences. When you are confronted with the task of proving the workability of some policy or course of action, the inductive process may be used if that policy or course of action has had widespread adoption and use in the past. Humankind has come to accept universal laws and truths because of the frequent inductive verification of them. For example, "All humans die" and "Democracy preserves the greatest amount of freedom

for humankind." You will find induction a valuable tool in developing propositions of a similar nature.

INDUCTION DEFINED

Inductive reasoning is the process of studying a sufficient number of analogous factual examples, finding a common characteristic, and naming it as a
general law or truth. A simpler definition would be: Inductive reasoning is the
process of citing a sufficient number of specific examples to prove a generalization. Although you should never define induction with the following words,
you may characterize the process as "going from the specific to the general."

In this case you cite factual example one, example two, and so on, until a
sufficient number has been cited. Then you draw the conclusion, which is a
generalized statement about those factual examples. You may also reverse the
process. You may state the generalization that you intend to prove and then
cite the factual examples that support it.

In both cases you are using the inductive process.

CHARACTERISTICS OF INDUCTION

There are certain characteristics that you should remember about inductive
reasoning:

1. *The examples cited or studied must be factual;* they did occur; they did
   happen. They cannot be hypothetical.

2. *The examples must be analogous;* they must be of the same type, species,
   or category. One may prove certain generalized truths about horses, but
   hardly from an example of one horse, and certainly not from a piece of coal,
   a lake, or a stone.

3. *The induction must be built on a sufficient number of factual examples.*
   What constitutes a sufficient number is relative, depending on the nature
   of your subject and your audience. If the category of things you are talking about, such as discrimination on the basis of gender, race, or sexual
   orientation, pertains to the whole United States, it is insufficient to cite
   examples from the state of Georgia alone. An audience that has knowledge of the ramifications of your subject will usually require more examples than one that has little. An audience that does not want to believe

your conclusion will demand more examples than an audience that does want to believe.

4. *The conclusion of induction is a generalization;* it is a statement about those factual examples as a class; it states a characteristic that those factual examples have in common. The conclusion will never be stated in terms of "Jim," "Sally," or the racehorse, "Secretariat."

The foregoing characteristics are suggested by the definition. Two more you should be aware of:

5. *Inductive reasoning usually involves an "inductive leap."* To reason inductively, we seldom study all the examples in existence in the world; we study only a sufficient number, a sample. To assume that what is true for the sample will be true for all cases is the "inductive leap" involved. Many of the fallacies of this kind of reasoning center around this inductive leap.

6. *All induction is based on facts;* therefore, all the principles and lines of argument on facts apply to induction. Whenever we talk of *percentages, ratios, indexes, the majority of cases,* and the *minority of cases,* we are using statistical terms. Yet for most subjects that we are apt to become advocates for and use such statistical terms, the probabilities are great that the actual statistics have been gathered by a sampling process (an inductive process) rather than the complete "counting of noses." Remember that a complete census is taken only once every 10 years in the United States. The information gathered is eventually published in several volumes of statistical tables. Many of those tables are based on a sampling process rather than consideration of all the examples.

THE USE OF INDUCTION IN DISCOVERING OR VERIFYING KNOWLEDGE

People constantly search for new knowledge—seeking to see if conditions have changed, seeking to verify hypotheses. This quest uses various research methods, many of which are based on induction or are closely related to it. Let us consider these.

Induction and the Sampling Process

A research worker in the field of social science will often use a sampling process to find out information about people. Often in such surveys (sampling process) a very small percentage of the total of society will be noted, and we conclude what was true for these few will be true for the many. Some examples of information gathered in the sampling process include: incomes of the various professions, working conditions, hours of work, what people are wearing, what people are watching on TV, and what portion of the people are educated. In books of statistics, accordingly, the statistics given are based on a sampling rather than on the complete counting of all the examples possible. This sampling process is used everywhere. It was used in medicine to verify that penicillin can cure certain diseases. It is used in the world of agriculture to verify the best methods of growing crops or preventing soil erosion. Thus, whenever you read facts you should be aware of the possibility that they may have been gained by the sampling process and knowing the sampling process will help you identify it as inductive reasoning.

Induction and Public Opinion Polls

Public opinion polls are the result of the sampling process. Because public speakers make such frequent use of them, they deserve a special word here. Polls are often used to indicate how candidates will fare in an election. The ways these samples are taken has much to do with the results. A poll of random citizens will be less accurate than a poll of registered voters (those not registered will not vote), and a poll of voters who intend to vote will be more accurate than a poll of registered voters (many registered voters will not vote). A sample that better represents the whole will be more accurate. At our university a poll was taken asking students were they satisfied with their classes showed a large percentage was satisfied. Later it was revealed that the survey had been taken at an event for graduating students. Obviously, those who were not satisfied were not adequately represented because they may have left the university or failed to graduate.

Another example would be any number of "polls" you see on various news web sites. They pose a question, suggest categories of answers, and invite visitors to vote online and view the results. These polls are not scientific because their sample populations are not carefully chosen. The polls appeal to people who have strong opinions about an issue (some may vote several times), survey only those who visit that web site, and have questions and categories that are improperly written. All reputable news web sites caution readers about making strong conclusions from these results. Students of argumentation should be wary of such polls and surveys if they are unrepresentative of the whole group supposedly being measured.

Sampling techniques have improved considerably, and although no sample can be entirely certain in its conclusion, the margin of error has been reduced. Criteria have been set up and a very small percentage of the people of the country who fit the criteria are asked their opinions. Based on their answers, the thinking of the American public is determined as a percentage figure. The announced percentages are subject to various levels of error because the size of the sample is small. Many felt that the mistakes made in the polls predicting the 2000 U.S. presidential election invalidated public opinion polls. This was untrue, those errors merely taught us that in propositions that are very close, the figures should probably be given as plus or minus 2 percent. Thus, when engaging in a sampling process, particularly of public opinion, proper methods must be used, the sample must be typical of that which is being sampled, and the possibilities of degree of error should be determined before reaching the final conclusion. Remember also that the sampling process in many other cases, including the most scientific of fields, uses only a few of the total examples possible.

Induction and the Case-Study Method

Another method that may be used to uncover knowledge is known as the case study, wherein the researcher makes a very definitive study of one particular example. An intensive study of one tree, one race horse, one stutterer, or the techniques of one evangelist, for example, is typical of this method and much information can be gleaned from such a study—the conclusions of which are similar to those drawn from the inductive process. The difference being that the conclusions are drawn from one case instead of several cases. The weakness of the case study is that conclusions are based on only one case, hardly sufficient for making a generalized conclusion. On the other hand, in the case study of a speaker, a particular technique may have been used a sufficient number of times to make possible a generalization using the inductive process. Often, however, additional studies using the case-study method will have been made and these may verify the truth of the conclusions drawn. Be aware, however, as users of argument, that the case-study method will support any inductive reasoning that we may be using in gaining the belief of audiences.

Induction and Experimental Study

In the social sciences, the experimental study is being used more and more widely to discover knowledge about humankind. This method is based on induction but uses a technique whereby the number of examples studied can be greatly reduced by use of a "control group." Suppose for a moment that we hold to the hypothesis that a course of argumentation taught in the university develops critical thinking. To prove this inductively we must have a sufficient number of cases (individuals whose critical thinking has been improved by such a course). To find these individuals, we would get a variety of colleges, perhaps 20, to participate in the experiment. We would give a critical thinking test to the students who expected to take such a course and to an equal number who did not. Concurrently, we would select a control group at each college. These control groups would consist of students who matched those taking the course in every significant way: by aptitude tests, by sex, by interests, and by courses taken. Matching them as nearly as possible would reduce the variations between the two groups to only one—those in the experimental group would be individuals taking the course, while those in the control group would be those not taking the course. At the conclusion of the course, another critical thinking test would be administered to both the experimental and the control groups. If the experimental group, those taking the argumentation course, achieved higher grades on the test than those not taking it, we could draw the conclusion from such an inductive process that a course of argumentation in the university does develop critical thinking. The test of critical thinking would have to be verified as actually measuring critical thinking; another step would be to administer a test again, two or more months after the course, to see if the improvement was permanent.

This method of research is being used more and more in the field of the social sciences. In the field of speech, such studies have increased our knowledge about the rehabilitation of those with speech disorders. Such studies have increased our knowledge of the art of persuasion and taught us much about radio and television. Because of this kind of research, we know that the chemistry of the blood of the stutterer is different and that the incidence of stuttering among twins is greater. We know that one individual can persuade another who is alone with her more easily than if they were in a larger audience.

Induction and the Empirical Method

Much of the knowledge that humankind has gleaned from the world has been achieved by what is known as the "empirical method." In the preceding chapter on evidence, we learned that an authority in a field is one who is trained in research, who has made a study, who avoids exaggeration, and who is free from prejudice. We also ask that she has made a formal study of the subject on which she is testifying. The empirical method will violate many of these criteria. The empirical method has a key, but objective, observer reporting his observations. We can and do give a good deal of credence to individuals who are not trained in research but who are capable of reporting knowledge to us. Our outstanding sports stars who have spent many years in a particular game have much knowledge to give us about their sport. A racehorse trainer who has been successful in training winning horses is listened to with respect, as is a United States senator who has been too busy to make a formal research study. Such individuals, having lived long enough to make many observations about baseball players, race horses, or aspects of government, have informally made an inductive survey of the subject about which they speak. Their conclusions are usually based on many observations and will meet the tests of good inductive reasoning. Thus, knowledge gained by the empirical method, based as it often is on an informal inductive survey, is both reliable and noteworthy.

Induction and Universal Laws

Humans have come to accept many universal laws and principles about which no formal research study has ever been made. These laws or principles have been inductively proved many times, and, because they have, we accept them as being true. We accept the truth, "All humans die," on the grounds that most of us have seen sufficient examples to believe this truth. In a similar fashion, we are quite convinced that rain will make us wet, that falling objects may hurt us, and that water will quench our thirst. In each of these cases we believe because we have had a sufficient number of examples to prove it to us. In the same fashion, we have come to believe in certain principles or rules of conduct. We believe that honesty is the best policy, that work is essential for accomplishment, that consideration and respect for others is the basis of winning friends. Here again enough people have observed a sufficient number of examples so that we have come to believe these principles. The inductive process has established many premises on which we build other forms of reasoning. Induction has played a very important role in establishing the beliefs of humankind. The wise speaker is quick to discern those principles or universal laws that humankind has accepted, She is also quick to discern those that may need inductive proof and proceeds to furnish it whenever the audience may demand it.

Induction has played an important role in helping us to discover or to verify the knowledge of the world. Whenever a researcher is using a sampling process, he is using the inductive method; the case-study method adds another strong example to verify a conclusion; experimental studies, in the social sciences as well as the physical sciences, verify hypotheses by using an inductive process—those who are experienced in various walks of life may reveal to us important knowledge by means of the empirical method, a method that may have induction at its base; universal laws or principles have resulted from the observations of many people observing a sufficient number of examples to draw the conclusions in the form of those universal laws or principles. These are the ways that humankind makes use of induction to uncover knowledge of the world or to verify it.

LINES OF ARGUMENT TO VALIDATE OR INVALIDATE INDUCTION

Whenever the speaker or writer is using induction to influence others, she will need to make sure that the inductive process used is valid and acceptable. To do so, she uses lines of argument that validate the conclusion drawn. A listener or reader who wants to refute a conclusion needs lines of argument that invalidate the inductive conclusions of others. The following lines of argument are those that validate, test, or invalidate the inductive process.

Are the Facts True?

Sound induction must be based on examples that are factual, examples that did occur. It cannot be based on hypothetical examples or the supposition that something might have happened. If you wish to validate your inductive process, you must utilize the lines of argument discussed earlier. You can point out that the factual examples cited were gathered by a person trained in research, one who made a very definite study of the subject, and one who was free from prejudice and free from exaggeration.

You also have available to you the various lines of argument on statistics, including that the statistics are an accurate index for what you want to prove and that examples gathered from other sources verify these uncovered by this particular researcher. You may make your inductive process more believable if you make sure that your listeners are convinced that the facts are true. On the other hand, if you wish to test the conclusion of the speaker, or if you wish to refute her, you may use the same lines of argument in the opposite fashion to invalidate the induction. You can suggest that the examples cited were not gathered by a person trained in research or in observation, or that they were gathered by an individual who is prejudiced or who likes to exaggerate by choosing only the extremes. You can point out that these examples, if they are cited as percentages or total statistics or ratios, are not really an index to what we want to know or that the examples are not comparable. Thus the first line of argument by which you validate or invalidate induction is to ask whether the examples are factual, and in so doing you have available all the lines of argument on evidence.

Are the Examples Universal or Isolated Instances?

Whenever you are trying to influence by using the inductive process, you should leave the impression that the examples you are citing or could cite are universal rather than isolated instances. If you are trying to convince an audience, for example, that organized crime is widespread, use Boston, New York, Chicago, San Francisco, Los Angeles, New Orleans, or other large cities as examples. If all your examples revolve about one area or one city, you can readily be accused of using isolated examples or your opponent can contend that your conclusion is unsound because examples of organized crime are not widespread. In speaking of a national problem, you must leave the impression that the statement is true in all parts of the country. If you are trying to test or refute the inductive process, a powerful line of argument is to reveal that the speaker was able to cite only isolated instances. Often suggesting that these cases are exceptional can achieve that end. For example, you can suggest that, of all the people involved, the percentage who are organized criminals is very small. Use percentages if they are available; you can often show that the problem is less dire than it has been pictured. This line of argument used either to validate or invalidate is based on the principle that the conclusion drawn from the inductive process is a generalization. This fallacy of drawing a universal conclusion from too few examples is known as "hasty generalization."

Do the Examples Cover a Sufficient Period of Time?

Whenever the least possibility arises that time is a factor in your inductive conclusion, you must make sure that your audience sees not only that your examples cover a wide area but also that they are spread out in time. This is quite obvious whenever you are trying to prove inductively a proposition that establishes a trend. To reveal to an audience that the United States government has increasingly favored deregulation, you must show examples over a period of two or three decades. However, many other propositions may be floated in which time may not seem to be a factor at first. With a proposition in which you are attempting to show that organized crime is a problem, you will strengthen your argument if you demonstrate that it is a problem of considerable duration.

The effectiveness of this line of argument to validate your induction is readily observed in proving the proposition: "The problem of lynching has been a meaningful part of United States history." To prove that this was a continuing problem in the mid-twentieth century, you could cite the number of lynchings in various decades. The World Almanac, drawing from the Department of Records and Research of Tuskegee Institute in Alabama, reveals that in 1900 a total of 115 lynchings occurred; in 1910, 76; in 1920, 61; in 1930, 21; and 1935, the last year of any significant number, saw 20. By 1940 the number was down to 5 and by 1950 there were only about 2 lynchings per year. From these statistics, covering a period of 50 years, the conclusion may be drawn that lynching was a problem in the United States. Note that when a longer time is covered, the argument is considerably strengthened. Of course, any lynching is one too many.

In evaluating or refuting induction, this line of argument can be quite effective. If you can reveal that the examples cited were all taken from one year and that they happened two or three years ago, you nullify to a great degree the effectiveness of the speaker's argument. In areas in which conditions change quite rapidly, such as in the sciences, this is particularly true. The technique is to point out what might be expected of a speaker whose argument is sound and that the speaker has failed to convince us with the cases cited.

Are the Examples Cited Typical or Atypical?

Great extremes exist everywhere in this world. People vary in intelligence from the idiot to the genius. Storms vary from those gentle ones that leave only a trace of rainfall to disastrous hurricanes or tornadoes. People's attitudes vary from the ultraconservative to the ultraliberal. This variation in occurrences is often represented by a bell-shaped curve when illustrated on a graph.

So much do people and occurrences vary that suggesting that a typical person exists or that an occurrence might be typical can be difficult. Often you will need to suggest that your chosen examples are typical because they do make a proper sampling from the ultraconservative to the ultraliberal or from the weakest type of storm to the most severe. Choose your examples wisely to increase the belief of the audience in your conclusion.

The evaluator will be very careful to test whether a speaker has chosen typical examples and will adjust her thinking accordingly. The person who is refuting will be quick to know and point out that the examples are atypical if they are. That citing typical examples is difficult gives an advantage to the refuter in making a counterargument. So, for example, your opponent might readily charge that the examples of crime among young people you have cited are atypical because so many young people do not commit criminal acts.

This line of argument can be used on many other propositions about which one may be drawing inductive conclusions.

Are There Significant Negative Instances?

Induction is the process of demonstrating that a certain characteristic exists among the members of a particular category of things. The process is one of showing that the characteristic is generally true of all the examples. Whenever the characteristic is absent from one of the examples, we have what is known as a "negative instance." These negative instances become the exceptions to the rule. A negative instance, then, can be defined as an example within a category of things in which the characteristic or the general rule does not occur. The old saying, "Exceptions prove the rule," is quite false. Exceptions, or negative instances, disprove the rule. The more frequent the exceptions, the more doubtful any conclusion drawn. A student of logic is quite aware of the necessity of studying the number of times exceptions occur and of drawing his conclusions on the basis of those exceptions. For example, at one time in the study of stuttering researchers believed that cerebral dominance in the form of handedness played an important role. They thought that people who were forced to write with the right hand when they really should have been using the left hand were disturbed in such a way as to bring about stuttering. So many exceptions to the rule were found, however, that they had to change their conclusions considerably. In fact, they discovered that this was true in just under 20 percent of the cases, while in better than 80 percent (the exceptions), it was irrelevant. Thus, the conclusion that this was true in all cases had to be modified to the conclusion that it was probably true in a small, yet significant, minority of cases. The negative instances caused researchers to change their beliefs.

As a speaker, when you are trying to prove something inductively and you know there are few or no negative instances, you can strengthen your argument considerably. If you know that what you are talking about is true and can claim without exception that it occurs, you have the strongest possible inductive proof. That no exceptions have been found to the rule that humans die compels us to believe that all humans must die. Physical laws are often good examples of this sort of induction: rain causes wetness; if I drop a piece of chalk in my argumentation class, it will fall because of gravity; a person cannot be in two places at the same time; and light allows a person to see. Even if very rare exceptions are possible (if my argumentation class is being conducted in the International Space Station, for example) or even if a statement is only true in 95 instances out of 100, inductions of this sort can be very persuasive to audiences.

You can often build an argument on the basis of its significance, maintaining that although something happens rarely, when it does happen, it is of great importance. Many of our laws regulating human conduct are based on this argument. Murder, for instance, is not the behavior of the majority; in fact, only an exceptional minority are ever involved in it. Even though less than 1 percent of humankind have or would engage in it, that percentage is significant enough for us to have strong laws and set up as effective a police force as possible to prevent and to punish it. Thus, when as a speaker you show inductively that a certain thing occurs even in a small number of cases, that number may be significant. The process here is to show why even that small number is significant. Those who supported anti-lynching legislation did so on the grounds that even one person lynched is a horrible crime and should be prevented by every means possible.

The person who would test and evaluate or refute the arguments of another will find the citation of negative instances a most powerful tool. If you are in this situation and can show case after case in which the thing did not happen universally, you have a powerful means of gaining belief. To be successful, however, requires you to have a rather thorough knowledge of the area being discussed. Often as we sit in an audience and listen to speakers, we don't have enough knowledge of the number of negative instances to know whether the speaker's induction is true or not. We may be misled because we don't know how often exceptions occur. In listening to the speeches of your fellow students, you may find yourself confronted with this problem. Citing what exceptions you do know will assist you whenever you are called on to evaluate their arguments.

This method of evaluation or refutation could be called a "quantitative approach." Applying this to the number of pedophiles who are priests, you should look up the total number of priests in the United States, then contrast the number found to be pedophiles with the total number of priests. As the number found will be a small percentage, you can minimize the problem using the line of argument that the differences are not great enough to demand any change or new solution. This is a particularly effective tool against those speakers who tend to exaggerate and leave the impression that the atypical and worst cases are the usual. We remember an occasion when this line of argument was used quite effectively in refutation. An affirmative team had been charging that oligopolies were guilty of price fixing. The speaker on the negative, using a statistical handbook, revealed case after case where the prices had varied and were not fixed. She cited so many examples that she left the impression that oligopolies changed prices according to changing conditions rather than fixed them at a constant level. Thus, the line of argument that there are or are not significant negative instances becomes a powerful means of influencing belief.

Is the Conclusion Properly Stated?

Many using argument tend to draw conclusions that they would like from specific examples rather than those that they can draw logically. Betrayed by their prejudices, these people state a conclusion different from what could be logically stated. For example, an individual prejudiced against modern capitalism might cite the examples of very low incomes and unusually high incomes and draw the conclusion that in the United States income is distributed unfairly. When examining such statistics, the only proper conclusion that can be drawn is that income in the United States is distributed unequally. For the speaker to arrive at the conclusion that such a disparity of incomes is unfair would require considerable additional proof. Thus, the student of argument should be very careful to study the examples cited or available for citation to see exactly what generalized conclusion can be drawn from them. Do not fall into the temptation of overstating the case.

In using induction to build an argument, the speaker will be more likely to gain belief if she states her conclusion accurately. Understatement is psychologically better than overstatement. The speaker who overstates tends to get a "no response." The speaker who tends to understate may often lead the audience to draw the strong conclusion that she desires. She achieves her goal by creating the impression of fairness. Thus, the speaker who states accurately the proper conclusion will tend to gain a fair hearing; she who exaggerates may lead her audience into believing that her argument is fallacious.

The ability to state the proper conclusions as an evaluator or refuter is desirable. Consider some of the examples cited at the end of the last chapter. American Automobile Association reports show that Nevada spends more per capita on roads than New York; obviously Nevada must have better roads than New York. The conclusion is just as obviously misstated. The only proper conclusion that can be drawn from the evidence cited is that Nevada spends more per capita on roads than New York. Any other conclusion is hardly warranted. In the study of stutterers, Professor Mildred Berry states the conclusion rather accurately when she suggests, "there must be a relationship between stuttering and twinning." This statement is not overdrawn and the unknowns in this situation are left in the zone of the unknown. Thus, in induction, whenever you have a variety of examples cited, try to develop the skill of being able to point out such conclusions. The process is one of stating the conclusion that the speaker has drawn and then explaining how the examples cited warrant only the particular conclusion that you state.

The "What Harm?" or "So What?" Argument

Anything that is harmful to us or decreases our chances to earn a livelihood, that prevents us from obtaining food, clothing, and shelter, that alienates friends, or destroys our freedoms of speech, press, and religion, concerns us. In Chapter 1 we pointed out that most arguments, particularly the strongest ones, are rooted in the emotions. In building most arguments, we must first establish the truth of the argument and then reveal its significance—we prove that it exists and then we prove that it concerns us.

This particular argument is both inductive and deductive. It is inductive in that it must be shown that the things we are talking about are widespread. Thus, if we say that a certain evil exists, we must show that it is widespread enough and prevalent enough to concern us. This argument is deductive because the advocate must reveal that some form of harm is occurring because of its presence. The assumption is made that anything that harms another is bad and that this particular thing being talked about harms us and therefore is an evil. The speaker desiring more money for education must prove that lack of funds is widespread and then that the lack of educational opportunities in the twenty first century is harmful. The speaker who would have us abolish the Electoral College has the task of showing the harm that the Electoral College does to the United States.

This particular argument becomes a powerful one for the individual who would evaluate or refute. You have a very effective argument in refuting if you can show that the thing being considered seldom occurs and when it does no one is harmed or at most little harm is done. This is both a quantitative and a qualitative argument. Quantitative with respect to frequency of occurrence, qualitative regarding the harm achieved by each occurrence. Pieces of falling satellites have rarely survived their reentry into the atmosphere, but when they do fall to Earth they have not injured humans.

This same line of argument can be used with reference to the advantages of new solutions or the objections to them. If new advantages fail to bring any significant improvement or if the alleged objections are insignificant, they can readily be refuted. Consider the following example: Those advocating recognition of a country by a national government point to the advantage of being able to sit down around the table and directly negotiate with that country. Those who would refute such an argument claim that the advantage is insignificant, particularly where authoritarian nations are concerned. They suggest that no good can come of sitting around the table and talking with representatives of a nation that is dedicated to the very opposite of a democratic family of nations. So, the person who refutes merely says in so many words, "All right, we can sit around the table and negotiate, so what? We get nowhere by doing it." Or consider another example of refuting an objection to a new proposal. Often those who oppose the government's taking on additional duties charge that this will lead to "big government." The "so what" argument applied and properly elaborated can be effective. "They tell us this will lead to 'big government.' What if it does? These new governmental programs are helping people in very basic areas of our lives. What is the harm of the government's doing it? What harm has come to the United States because the federal government has owned and operated the national parks? What harm has come from governments owning and operating the schools? What harm has come from our municipally owned and operated electric plants? Until the gentleperson shows that this type of government is a harmful thing we merely ask, 'so what'?"

Induction is a powerful weapon in influencing the belief of people. It is used by speakers to show that evils exist in the present system or that the present system has significant advantages, to show historical trends, to estimate public opinion, to show that courses of action that have had widespread use are advantageous, and to establish universal truths. We have noted the characteristics of induction: that it is factual, that the examples cited are analogous, that it must be built on a sufficient number of examples, that the conclusion is a generalization. We have also noted that induction is used widely in all areas of endeavor for uncovering knowledge and verifying findings. It is the basis of the sampling method of public opinion polls, of the case study method, of the experimental study, or the empirical method. It is the great verifier of our universal laws. Thus, a student who wishes to become an effective in influencing others through argument will learn its use and will particularly develop his skill in the various lines of argument by which he can either strengthen his arguments by making them sound more valid or be able to refute the arguments of others. Those of you who achieve these will find induction a strong tool for gaining belief.

EXERCISES

1. Define:
   a. Induction
   b. A sample
   c. Validate
   d. Invalidate

2. Explain what is meant by each of the following characteristics of induction:
   a. The examples are factual.
   b. The examples must be analogous.
   c. The induction must be built on a sufficient number of examples.
   d. The conclusion is a generalization.
   e. It involves an "inductive leap."
   f. Much induction is based on statistics.

3. Explain what is meant by a sampling process.

4. How would you categorize the students on your campus to get an accurate public opinion poll from them on student affairs?

5. Under what tests of induction might the case study be more likely to fail?

6. Outline in detail some experimental study that might be of interest to you that would uncover new knowledge.

7. Why is a person at age 50 more likely to have sound conclusions from empirical data than a person at the age of 25? Explain in terms of induction.

8. What is meant by the following?
   a. Universal example
   b. Isolated instances
   c. Typical examples
   d. Atypical examples
   e. Negative instances

9. The following are attempts at inductive reasoning. Explain why each is inductive; use lines of argument to evaluate or refute.

a. Mary Smith is tall; Jack Smith is tall; Frank Smith is tall. The Smith family must be a tall family.

b. The percentage of native born New Yorkers living in New York City must be very small. Last Saturday evening I stopped 100 individuals as they were walking down the street past Times Square. Only one was a native of New York City.

c. I shall never like Tim Johnson. I was introduced to him the other night and he insulted my sweetheart.

d. Professor Smith is better known than Professor Jones. The other day I stood in the hall of the science building with pictures of each. Twice as many were able to identify Professor Smith as Professor Jones.

e. She is a social boor. I was out to dinner with her the other night and she left her spoon in the coffee cup.

f. Banks are untrustworthy and all bankers are swindlers. Why, I lost $1,000 to a banker once.

g. Oh, she is nothing but a drunkard! I had a date with her and she got very intoxicated.

h. You can see from the papers that all they do in college is play football and basketball.

i. She must be an ignorant person. She didn't know but 24 state capitals out of the 50. She could only name 15 of our presidents. She could name only cities with a population of over a million persons.

j. Indiana certainly is a flat state. I went through it on my way to Chicago and I didn't see a single hill.

k. Income is unfairly distributed in country X. The government's own figures reveal to us that in 2000 the average farm worker got only $21,302 a year and the average schoolteacher received only $22,420. However, the average auto worker got $41,007 per year and the average security and commodity broker got as much as $68,163. In other words, there is an unfair distribution of income from profession to profession.

l. Pollution of our rivers is a serious problem in the United States. Studies by the Department of the Interior reveal that the Annacostia, the Potomac, the Ohio, and the Mississippi are particularly bad.

Chapter 7
Influencing Through Deduction

PROPOSITIONS WITH WHICH DEDUCTION IS EFFECTIVE

The overall context of the argument will be deductive when you are trying to gain the belief of others on such propositions as: "The evils of the present system are great enough to demand a change"; or, "The advantages or benefits of the old system are so great as to warrant its retention"; or, "The objections or dangers of the proposed system are too great to justify its adoption"; or, "The benefits or advantages of the new proposal warrant its adoption." Deduction may be your only available method on some propositions of future probability. It is available to you in propositions conditioned by an "if" clause and in those cases when alternative choices confront you. Before we can fully understand, we must first know what deductive reasoning is.

DEDUCTIVE REASONING DEFINED

Deductive reasoning is that form of reasoning in which a conclusion is drawn from premises. The following are examples of deductive reasoning, but are not necessarily free from fallacies:

1. *Proposition of value:*

Any form of government that destroys freedom of speech and freedom of press, and does not allow the people to elect their own representatives, is a bad form of government.

Totalitarianism destroys freedom of speech and freedom of press, and does not allow the people to elect their own representatives.

Therefore, totalitarianism is a bad form of government.

2. *Proposition of past fact:*

Any state that has good roads has good appropriations for them.

California has good roads.

Therefore, California has had good appropriations for them.

3. *Proposition of future probability:*

Any person who has a record of honesty in the past can be relied on to be honest in the future.

John Jackson has a record of honesty in the past.

Therefore, John Jackson can be relied on to be honest in the future.

Note that the proposition to be proved in each case is the concluding statement of the deduction.

In each of the above examples the conclusion is drawn from the two statements that precede it. The first two statements are the premises on which the conclusion is based.

THE SYLLOGISM AND ITS PARTS

"Syllogism" is the name given to that form of deduction in which both premises and the conclusion are stated for the listener or reader. All three statements are clearly expressed and present, as in the examples above. The first statement of the syllogism is called the "major premise," the second statement is called the "minor premise," and the last statement is called the "conclusion."

Major premise: Humans die.

Minor premise: You are a human.

Conclusion: Therefore, you will die.

If you will examine the above syllogism more closely, you will notice still other features about it; you will notice that it can be broken into parts even further. It can be expressed mathematically:

$A = B$

$C = A$

Therefore, $C = B$

A (Humans) B (die)

C (You) A (are a human)

C (You) B (will die)

The term *die* (B) appears in both the major premise and the conclusion and is called the "major term." The term *you* appears in the minor premise and the conclusion and is called the "minor term." The term *human* appears in both the major and minor premises and is the means by which the minor term is brought together with the major term to form the conclusion. It is called the "middle term" because it is the way by which the major term is joined with the minor term. Thus the parts of the syllogism are:

Major premise: (middle term) Humans die (major term).

Minor premise: (minor term) You are a human (middle term).

Conclusion: (minor term) You will die (major term).

THE ENTHYMEME

Seldom does the writer or speaker make use of the three statements of the syllogism in presenting her deductive reasoning. One of the three statements is usually omitted. When deduction is used with only two of the statements present, we call it an "enthymeme." When we say, "You are a human; therefore, you will die," the major premise has not been stated. We may leave the minor premise unstated by saying, "Humans die; therefore, you will." Or we may sometimes leave out the conclusion by saying, "Humans die, and you are a human." Remember that whenever we, or anyone else, use the enthymemic form of deduction, we are assuming that the reasoning will gain belief without presenting the third statement.

However, to be able to test the soundness of deductive reasoning, either our own or that of another, we must develop skill in changing enthymemes into syllogisms. Only in the syllogistic form will we have maximum opportunity to examine both premises and conclusion. Let us change the enthymeme, "The present system has three evils; therefore it should be abolished," into a syllogism. We get:

Any system with three evils should be abolished.

The present system has three evils.

Therefore, it should be abolished.

In the enthymeme the major premise has not been stated. Changing the enthymeme into a syllogism provides us an opportunity to discover one of the probable fallacies in the reasoning. Anyone would quickly doubt the major premise once it is stated. The key to changing enthymemes into syllogisms is recognition that all three terms of the syllogism—but not all three statements—will be present in the enthymeme. The first step is to analyze the enthymeme to determine which of the three statements is missing. Then, by remembering that the major premise contains the middle and major terms, that the minor premise contains the minor and middle terms, and that the conclusion contains the minor and major terms, you can put the syllogism together. In the example above, the word *therefore* immediately identifies the conclusion for you and thus the minor and major terms. Since the word *it* is the minor term in the conclusion, we can readily perceive that "it" refers to "the present system," and we have identified the minor premise with the middle term of *has three evils*. From this the major premise can be pieced together. A similar process is used in case either of the other two statements has been omitted.

TYPES OF DEDUCTION

Three kinds of deduction are available to you: categorical, disjunctive, and hypothetical.

Categorical Deduction

You will probably use this type more frequently than either of the others. Categorical deduction demonstrates that a general law or truth applies to a specific instance. The major premise is an assertion applied to a large category of persons, places, or things. The minor premise asserts that a specific case or instance is a part of the category indicated in the major premise. The conclusion asserts that what is true for the whole category will be true for the particular case. The descriptive phrase—"going from the general to the specific"—used by some to define deduction, suggests the process of categorical deduction, but it is an incomplete definition because it does not include the disjunctive and hypothetical. It is not a definition; it is merely descriptive of the process.

The True or Proved Major Premise Versus the False or Unproved. The major premise of categorical deduction must either be immediately acceptable to the audience or be proved. If it is a general truth that will be readily accepted by the audience, you need not prove it. For example, the premise, "All humans die." If, however, the audience won't accept your premise, then you must prove it. Most frequently this will require inductive proof. "All humans die" has been inductively proved throughout the ages. If a causal relationship exists in the major premise, you may use that form of reasoning—in some cases you may use reasoning from analogy or you may establish the premise by documentary evidence. Thus, if you are using categorical deduction to gain the belief of audiences, you must make certain that they will believe the major premise.

If you are evaluating or refuting deduction, you may claim that the major premise is false or that it has not been proved true by induction or some other method of reasoning. Probably the best method of so doing is to enumerate for the audience what the speaker will have to do to prove it and why she won't be able to. If the major premise requires induction, you may use the lines of argument for induction. If causal reasoning is required to prove the major premise, then use it. The same is true if reasoning from analogy or evidence is required to establish the truth of the major premise. For example, the anticommunist crusade in the United States after World War II was based, in part, on the belief that "all members of the Communist Party believe in the forceful overthrow of the government." To reveal the weakness in this premise, a speaker could say, "The gentleperson has based his reasoning on the doubtful premise that all members of the Communist Party believe in the forceful overthrow of the government. Many of them may believe that. However, until the gentleperson produces evidence taken from a survey covering a sufficient number of members of the party, a sample, which shows that without exception all members believe in forceful overthrow, he has based her deduction on an unproved assumption. Until he does this, his argument is unworthy of our belief." If you can go ahead and show exceptions, your refutation will be that much more powerful.

The True or Proved Minor Premise Versus the False or Unproved. The minor premise of categorical deduction must be proved unless the audience will accept it as true without proof. More often than not, the minor premise will require proof and may constitute the bulk of the proof for the deduction. The following example is typical of deduction involved in proving propositions of policy:

Anything that will increase industrial production without bringing serious disadvantages or trouble should be mandated.

Eliminating unionized labor will increase industrial production without bringing serious disadvantages or trouble.

Therefore, eliminating unionized labor should be mandated.

Many in most audiences will readily accept the major premise of this deduction. The bulk of your time will be devoted to proving the minor premise, which will require a combination of various types of reasoning to gain the belief of the audience on it. In other cases your job will be simpler:

Vermont is a politically liberal state.

John Jackson is a Vermonter.

Therefore, John Jackson is probably a liberal.

To prove the minor premise in this deduction is easier. A document from the town clerk where John Jackson votes or his parents vote, if he is a minor, will be all that is required. Thus, if you want your deductive reasoning to be believed, you must prove your minor premise if you have reason to think that it won't be believed.

A line of argument that can be used to evaluate or refute deduction is to claim that the minor premise is false or at least not established as true. This can be done by proving the contrary to be true or by demonstrating to the audience what evidence and/or what arguments the speaker or writer would have to produce or develop for the minor premise to be worthy of belief.

Distribution Versus Lack of Distribution of Terms. Even if the major and minor premises are true, the conclusion may be false because of lack of distribution of the terms within the syllogism. This occurs in two ways. The first: not all members of the category designated have the attribute asserted. This lack of distribution is present whenever there may be exceptions to the general rule stated. Thus the specific instance may fall outside the general rule. For example:

Al-Qaeda believes in the destruction of the capitalist system.

John Jones is a member of Al-Qaeda.

Therefore, John Jones believes in the forceful overthrow of the capitalist system.

This deduction is quite sound if all members of Al-Qaeda believe in the forceful overthrow of the capitalist system. If there are exceptions, the reliability of the deduction is weakened because John Jones might be an exception.

As it is doubtful that 100 percent of the members of Al-Qaeda believe in the forceful overthrow of the capitalist system, and as we cannot be sure into which of the two classes John Jones falls, doubt is raised about the truth of the conclusion. Al-Qaeda may oppose many facets of Western societies, but capitalism may not be one of them. The probabilities may favor its truth, yet doubt remains. Here is another example of this type of fallacy:

Utah is a conservative state.

Mary Smith is from Utah.

Therefore, Mary Smith is probably a conservative.

This deduction is possibly fallacious because Mary Smith could readily be a moderate or belong to one of the other ideologies on the political spectrum. You can discover this fallacy by placing the word *all* at the beginning of the major premise or term. If the word *all* makes the premise false, then this fallacy is present. The terms have not been distributed properly.

Lack of distribution also occurs in those cases in which the attribute suggested by the major premise is not confined to the category designated by the syllogism. For example:

Terrorists believe in the destruction of property to achieve political aims.

The Animal Liberation Front believes in the destruction of property to achieve political aims.

Therefore, members of the Animal Liberation Front are terrorists.

This syllogism might be sound if only terrorists believed in that principle. As many others believe it also, the conclusion is fallacious. You can discover this particular fallacy by placing the word *only* at the beginning of the premise or term. If the word *only* makes the premise false, this fallacy is present. The premise, "Only terrorists believe in the destruction of property to achieve political aims," is obviously false.

Thus, to have sound deduction, you must make sure that no term is distributed in the conclusion unless it has been distributed properly in the premises. Be careful to avoid making wider application of the term in the conclusion than is warranted by the premises. Don't overstate your conclusion. For example:

> The Animal Liberation Front believes in direct action to disrupt corporations that mistreat animals.
>
> George Johnson believes in direct action to disrupt corporations that mistreat animals.
>
> Therefore, George Johnson believes in one of the principal tenets of the Animal Liberation Front.

Such a conclusion is warranted, while the conclusion "Therefore, George Johnson is a member of the Animal Liberation Front," is not. Psychologically, you will be better off avoiding the overstatement and the "no response" that it may bring. The same principle is true in those cases in which the word *all* would make the premise false.

The fallacy of lack of distribution of terms. Lack of distribution is that error in deduction in which one or more of the terms is given a wider application in the conclusion than is warranted from the premises. A term is distributed when the whole of it is referred to universally.

An **illicit major** is that fallacy of deduction in which the major term is given wider application in the conclusion than is warranted from its use in the major premise.

> Cats are animals.
>
> Dogs are not cats.
>
> Therefore, dogs are not animals.

This is fallacious because the major term *animals* in the conclusion is used in the universal sense of all animals, while in the major premise the word animals means only some animals.

An **illicit minor** is that fallacy of deduction in which the minor term is given wider application in the conclusion than is warranted by its use in the minor premise.

> All judges are trained in law.
>
> All judges are citizens.
>
> Therefore, all citizens are trained in law.

Again, in this case the minor term *citizens* in the minor premise refers only to some citizens, but in the conclusion it is used in the sense of all citizens.

The **undistributed middle** is that fallacy of deduction in which the middle term has not been used at least once in a universal sense.

The people of India are Asians.

Asians are Orientals.

Therefore, the people of India are Orientals.

In neither the major nor the minor premise has the middle term *Asians* been used to mean all Asians. In both cases Asians means some not all. In both the following examples the fallacy of undistributed middle occurs:

Al-Qaeda believes in the forceful overthrow of the government of Saudi Arabia.

John Jones is a member of Al-Qaeda.

Therefore, John Jones believes in the forceful overthrow of the government of Saudi Arabia.

As it is probably true that not all members of Al-Qaeda believe in the forceful overthrow of the government of Saudi Arabia, the middle term *Al Qaeda* has not been distributed universally in the major premise.

Democrats believe in national health care coverage.

Mary Brown believes in national health care coverage.

Therefore, Mary Brown is a Democrat.

In this case the middle term *believes in national health care coverage* has not been distributed universally in either premise. In neither premise has that term been used with the meaning of "all those who believe." The key word in this case is *only*. If the major premise could still be true and at the same time be stated, "Only members of the Democratic Party believe in national health care coverage," then the middle term would be distributed properly.

Revealing the lack of distribution of terms. Once you have discovered that some term in the deduction of some writer or speaker has not been distributed properly, the process of revealing it to the audience will prove difficult if you try to do it in the vocabulary of logic. Your average audience is unacquainted with the terms *illicit major* and *illicit minor*; the term *undistributed middle* would certainly conjure a mental image different from the one you intended. Certain lines of argument and certain sentences can reveal this fallacy to an audience. You might say:

+ Since the specific case could be an exception to the general rule as stated in the major premise, the conclusion is unworthy of our belief.

+ Since this is true of only some, not all, her conclusion is unworthy of our belief. (Since it is true that only some, not all, Vermonters are liberals, there is a good reason to doubt that John Jackson is a liberal.)

+ Until the gentleperson can demonstrate that only the group mentioned is concerned [hold that attitude or the like], her argument is unworthy of our belief.

These are a few suggestions by which the fallacy of lack of distribution of terms may be shown to an audience.

Four Terms, or the Fallacy of Equivocation. To be sound, the syllogism must have only three terms. The following syllogism is obviously fallacious because it has four terms:

> The people of India are Asians.
>
> Chinese are Orientals.
>
> Therefore, the people of India are Orientals.

The same rule applies also to meaning. Sometimes a term may consist of the same words in the two places within the syllogism, but have two different meanings. When this occurs, the syllogism has four terms and it is fallacious.

> Cat is a monosyllable.
>
> A cat drinks milk.
>
> Therefore, a monosyllable drinks milk.

Cat in the major premise means the word *cat*. In the minor premise it refers to the cat as an animal. Thus, the syllogism has four terms and the conclusion is fallacious. Sometimes the double meaning is difficult to discern:

> Public nuisances are punishable by law.
>
> A barking dog is a public nuisance.
>
> Therefore, a barking dog is punishable by law.

Because both premises seem to be relatively true, at first glance we may accept the conclusion as true, particularly if our neighbor has a barking dog. Deeper analysis will reveal that the conclusion is false because the term *public nuisance* has been used with two different meanings. In the major premise, it is used in the legal sense, while in the minor premise it has the meaning of an irritant such as dust, poison ivy, or mosquitoes. (Notice that you could refute this particular syllogism by the lack of distribution line of argument by saying, "Some, not all." However, you can make the refutation more effective by concluding with the explanation of the double meaning.)

You will encounter many occasions in which it will be difficult to determine whether there are four terms. This will be particularly true in propositions of policy like the following:

Immoral conduct is punished by law.

Discrimination in employment on the basis of race, color, or creed is immoral.

Therefore, discrimination in employment on the basis of race, color, or creed should be punished by law.

At the time of this writing, the majority of the people of the world have been sufficiently convinced of this; many nations have laws mandating fair employment practices. Residents of such nations believe that the term *immoral conduct* constitutes but a single term in the syllogism. Others, particularly in the non-protecting states, believe that it has a double meaning and that the conclusion is unworthy of belief. Most people believe those premises as stated. The issue is does discrimination in employment on the basis of race, color, or creed have the same or similar meaning to immoral conduct (e.g., adultery, rape, and murder) that is punishable by law or does it have the same or similar meaning to immoral conduct (e.g., swearing, lust, deceit, and the like) that is not punished by law?

The foregoing is an example of the difficulty you may encounter in trying to discover whether this fallacy is present. Furthermore, we should note that this is but one line of reasoning involved in this proposition; other factors may constitute the basis for the beliefs of many people on the subject. It does indicate a line of reasoning available to an advocate for the proposition, however. It also indicates the refutation of the proposal. You will encounter this possibility of four terms in many propositions of policy and will need to develop skill in handling it.

The name given to the foregoing fallacy is "equivocation," which may be defined as an error in reasoning in which a word or term is used with two or more meanings in developing an argument. Not only does equivocation appear in deduction, it may also occur in induction, causal reasoning, or reasoning from analogy as well.

Negative Premises. No sound conclusion can be drawn from two negative premises. For inferences to be drawn, a relationship must exist between the two premises. Two negative premises merely deny the existence of such a relationship. If X is not Y, and if Y is not Z, no particular relationship or agreement has been established between X and Z. The following syllogism is similarly fallacious:

> Americans are not Asians.
>
> Europeans are not Americans.
>
> Therefore, Europeans are Asians.

After looking at the foregoing example, don't jump to the conclusion that by using the word *not* in the conclusion we can disavow the negative premises rule. The following example will show why:

> Americans are not Asians.
>
> Chinese are not Americans.
>
> Therefore, Chinese are not Asians.

A conclusion drawn from negative premises has no reliability. However, the mere presence of the words *not* or *no* does not necessarily make the premise negative. In the following example, the premises are not negative:

> Any chemical substance that is not a compound is an element.
>
> Gold is not a compound.
>
> Therefore, gold is an element.

To evaluate or refute a deduction based on two negative premises, you will find it insufficient to point out the rule to your audience. Your method will have to be one of pointing out the lack of relationship among the terms of the two premises. In many cases, you may suggest a variety of other conclusions that are equally valid. In the first example given above, you could suggest to your audience that the conclusion "Europeans are not Asians" is just as logical a conclusion from the syllogism as the one stated. Furthermore, it is supported by known facts.

Disjunctive Deduction

Frequently, people are confronted with alternate choices. This is particularly true in determining standards of conduct, exercising judgments of value, and finding solutions to problems. As an advocate of a particular solution, for example, you may wish to demonstrate its superiority. To do so, you might use disjunctive deduction. The process consists in citing two or more alternatives and then demonstrating the inferiority of all but the one of your choice. You may then go on to demonstrate the superiority of the one you are advocating. In the simplest form of disjunctive deduction, two alternatives are given in the major premise, the minor premise affirms or denies one of the alternatives, and the conclusion denies or affirms the other.

> For you to pass the course either you must study harder or the professor must become more lenient.
>
> The professor will not become more lenient.
>
> Therefore, you must study harder.

In this disjunctive deduction, the minor premise denies one alternative and the conclusion affirms the other. The opposite occurs in the following, i.e., the minor premise affirms, the conclusion denies:

> Either China or the United States will be the world's only economic superpower.
>
> The United States will be the world's only economic superpower.
>
> Therefore, China cannot be the world's only superpower.

Notice that the words *either* and *or* become the significant symbols by which you can identify disjunctive deduction.

In those cases where three or more choices are offered, the minor premise denies all but one, while the conclusion affirms the preferred choice.

> We can go to the movies, go to the dance, or stay home and watch television.

The movies and television will be dull.

Therefore, let us go to the dance.

Actually, in the full development of this argument, such as in a long speech or in the discussion of the group wondering what to do, each of the undesired alternatives appears as though it were a separate minor premise. Thus the reasoning becomes:

We can go to the movies, or go to the dance, or stay home and watch television.

The dance will be dull; staying home and watching television will be uninteresting.

Therefore, let us go to the movies.

In the case of a speech, the summary as contained in the conclusion of the argument may appear in approximately this form or it may contain only the last three statements, leaving out the major premise.

Using Disjunctive Deduction Effectively. The major premise of disjunctive deduction must have certain attributes if it is to be sound and worthy of belief. First, as we have already noted, it must contain two or more alternatives. Second, just as in categorical deduction, it must be proved to the audience if it is not already accepted. Third, it must contain all the possible alternatives. The major premise "Either China or the United States will be the world's only economic superpower is fallacious as other alternatives are possible, including the emergence of another economic giant. Fourth, the alternatives cited must be mutually exclusive. It must be impossible to accept two or more of the alternatives. The alternatives in the following major premise are not mutually exclusive because both could be accepted: "To reduce drug addiction, we must either pass laws bringing stricter enforcement or establish a better system of education for its prevention." The alternatives of China or the United States becoming the world's superpower are not necessarily mutually exclusive— they might become equals.

In building an argument using disjunctive deduction, certain suggestions may be of help. Frequently you may choose to state the major premise. It can be introduced by the more informal "We have two (or more) choices open to us." If necessary to gain the belief of the audience, you may prove your argument by evidence from authority or other forms of evidence or reasoning as dictated by the nature of the premise. Avoid the pitfall of other alternatives by including all significant ones, but be careful to leave out the improbable ones or the ones that the audience already rejects. Often these can be suggested and then dismissed by quick reference to the common reason for rejection. If the audience is unlikely to believe that the alternatives are mutually exclusive, you may have to utilize exposition or lines of argument to overcome their skepticism. Finally, be careful not to overstate your case.

The bulk of your argument will often consist of using various forms of reasoning to substantiate the minor premise (or premises if more than three alternatives are offered). This will be particularly true if the conclusion seems to follow inevitably, as in Patrick Henry's speech, "Liberty or Death," where he devoted most of his time to the impossibility of peace. He spent no time developing arguments showing that the colonies could win the war. On the other hand, you may devote considerable time to offering arguments and evidence to support the alternative stated in the conclusion. This is essential particularly in those cases in which the audience will be reluctant to accept the conclusion even after they have accepted your other premises.

Evaluating or Refuting Disjunctive Deduction. The first step in evaluating this form of deduction is to word the major premise. Only through the wording of the complete syllogism can you discover potential errors. Having done this, the following lines of argument are available to you:

False or unproved major premise. (Same as for categorical deduction.)

Other alternatives. To use this line of argument you may merely suggest to the audience the other possible alternatives that the speaker or writer failed to mention and that the conclusion is therefore not justified. On the other hand, you may wish to select one of the omitted ones as the most justifiable and then proceed to support it with evidence and reasoning.

Alternatives not mutually exclusive. To use this line, you suggest that the choices aren't mutually exclusive and then proceed with exposition, evidence, and reasoning to demonstrate that both choices are possible, that they overlap, or that neither or none is possible nor desirable.

False minor premise or premises. (Same as for categorical.)

Denial of alternative stated in conclusion. Muster arguments supported by reasoning and evidence against this alternative, or reveal through an evaluation process that the alternative has not been proved to be a desirable or a logical choice.

Hypothetical Deduction

Another type of deduction available to you is hypothetical deduction. The course of events of the world may be modified, limited, or changed by differing conditions. Because we are constantly seeking to understand the forces and the events of the past, and as we often attempt to predict or change future events, hypothetical deduction is a type of reasoning frequently used. By definition, hypothetical deduction is that form of deductive reasoning based on a major premise that expresses a hypothetical or conditional relationship of sign or causation. The key by which you can identify this major premise is the word *if*. The conditional or limiting clause begins with the word *if*. For example (predicting the future):

> If our captain cannot play tonight, we will lose the game.
>
> Our captain cannot play tonight.
>
> Therefore, we will lose the game.

Or again (past fact):

> If it had rained, the ground would have been wet.
>
> The ground was not wet.
>
> Therefore, it did not rain.

Rules for Hypothetical Deduction. There are two ideas expressed in the hypothetical syllogism. The first, in the conditional clause, is called the "antecedent"; the second is expressed as the result and called the "consequent." Using this nomenclature the rules can be stated as follows:

1. If the minor premise affirms the antecedent, the conclusion must affirm the consequent. This is the case in the first example given above.

2. If the minor premise denies the consequent, the conclusion must deny the antecedent. This is the type of hypothetical syllogism in the second example given above.

3. A conclusion drawn from a minor premise that denies the antecedent is not necessarily true. It has greater probability of fallacy than one affirming the antecedent.

> If Congress passes an extensive federal aid to education bill, our schools will improve.
>
> Congress will not pass such a bill.
>
> Therefore our schools will not improve.

Various other forces are at work to provide good and improved schools, thus this conclusion does not follow.

4. A conclusion drawn from a minor premise that affirms the consequent is not necessarily true. When the hypothetical deduction takes this form, the conclusion is more likely to be false.

> If an honor system is adopted, there will be less cheating on examinations.
>
> There is less cheating on examinations.
>
> Therefore, an honor system has been adopted.

As so many other causes or conditions may have brought about the reduction in cheating, the conclusion does not necessarily follow.

Using Hypothetical Deduction Effectively. You will make extensive use of hypothetical deduction. In all propositions of policy, hypothetical deduction underlies the gaining of the belief of the audience on three major issues:

> If we adopt this solution or course of action, will it remove the evils?
>
> If we adopt this solution or course of action, will it bring worthwhile benefits?
>
> If we adopt this solution or course of action, will it be free from new and dangerous objections?

Before presenting your arguments built on hypothetical deduction, test them with the four rules given above. They are more likely to be believed if those rules are followed. However, rules three and four can be violated in some cases and you will still be able to gain the belief of your audience. The following violates rule four, and yet it is relatively believable:

If it rained, the ground would be wet.

The ground is wet.

Therefore, it has rained.

This will become more believable particularly if you demonstrate that no other causes, such as sprinklers, floods, or the like, could have caused the ground to be wet. Thus, follow the four rules above whenever possible, but the third and fourth can be violated, particularly when other lines of argument or evidence will support the conclusion.

Evaluating or Refuting Hypothetical Deduction. The rules given above provide good tests for the validity of the argument and serve as a starting guide. Don't use the terminology of the preceding rules in front of an audience, however, when trying to evaluate or refute hypothetical deduction. The average audience would hardly know what you are talking about if you were to say, "His argument is not worthy of your belief because he has denied the antecedent in his minor premise."

The best way to evaluate or refute hypothetical deduction for audiences is to use the lines of argument available to you under causal reasoning. Within the major premise of all hypothetical deduction, either a direct or indirect causal relationship is stated or implied. Search out that causal relationship and determine its weaknesses by using the lines of argument explained in the chapter on causal reasoning.

SORITES

Not always does deduction occur with two premises and a conclusion. Sometimes the conclusion is drawn from three or more premises. When this occurs, we have a "sorites." A sorites may be defined as that form of deduction in which a conclusion is drawn from three or more premises. This differs from the syllogistic form in that the latter is a conclusion drawn from only two premises. Whenever we have a sorites, we have a chain of reasoning. The following is an example:

A is B All lawyers are humans.

B is C All humans are vertebrates.

C is D All vertebrates are animals.

D is E All animals are mortal.

Therefore

A is E All lawyers are mortal.

Actually, a sorites is an abbreviated form of syllogistic reasoning in that various statements of the syllogisms involved have been omitted. In the foregoing example, the sorites could be expanded into three syllogisms. For example, the first one would be:

A is B All lawyers are humans.

B is C All humans are vertebrates.

Therefore

A is C All lawyers are vertebrates.

The next syllogism would be:

All lawyers are vertebrates.

All vertebrates are animals.

Thus

All lawyers are animals.

For the purposes of testing, break the whole of a sorites down into its successive syllogisms. By so doing, you can make sure that the sorites is either free from fallacy or, if fallacies are within it, you can discover them more readily.

The last example cited under that portion of this chapter devoted to disjunctive deduction is actually a sorites. Its major premise is: "We can go to the movies, or go to the dance, or stay at home and watch television." We have then two minor premises: "The dance will be dull," and "Staying home and watching television will be uninteresting." This is followed by the single conclusion, "Therefore, let us go to the movies." You should be aware of the sorites, how to evaluate it, and how to point out the fallacies that may exist within it.

DEDUCTION IN ARGUMENTATIVE SPEECHES

The most important and most frequent use of deductive reasoning in speeches, particularly those that are classified as argumentative, is on the main issue level. In the chapter on analysis, we learned that to gain the belief of an audience, we must first discover the main issues. As issues, they are stated in the form of questions, but in building the speech they must be worded as assertions and become the premises on which the final overall conclusion of the speech is built. Let us consider some examples.

Proposition of Fact

The main issues in a murder trial are:

+ Was someone killed by another person?
+ Was that person who did the killing John Doe?
+ Did John Doe deliberately plan the killing (with malice aforethought)?
+ Was John Doe of sound mind when he planned the killing?

In the final speech of the prosecuting attorney to the jury, these issues, stated in the form of declarative sentences, become the premises on which the final conclusion is built. The overall syllogism is:

> Anyone who, while of sound mind and with malice aforethought, kills another person is guilty of murder in the first degree.
>
> John Doe, while of sound mind and with malice aforethought, killed a person.
>
> Therefore, John Doe is guilty of murder in the first degree.

Notice that the minor premise of the syllogism is really four premises in one, each of which must be proved by the prosecutor. The major premise is derived from the statutes of the state. The conclusion will follow if the premises are proved. Thus, in propositions of fact that contain more than one issue, the overall development of the speech is deductive. Simple propositions of fact involving only one issue may be established by using other forms of reasoning or evidence without necessitating deduction.

Proposition of Value

As has been noted in the chapter on analysis, criteria for evaluation are set up for these propositions. These become the issues to be proved; when stated as assertions and proved, they form a deductive chain of reasoning by which the judgment of value can be made. The syllogism on which the speech is built will approximate the following:

Any system that fulfills the criteria should be adjudged good.

This system fulfills the criteria.

Therefore, this system should be adjudged good.

Theoretically, to win the belief of an audience, an advocate must be able to win the belief on each issue. Because few systems are perfect, this is extremely difficult to do on propositions of value, particularly when you are facing strong opposition. Frequently, to win belief, you need merely demonstrate that the good outweighs the bad. Don't try to do the impossible; the above syllogism is sometimes impossible to establish completely. It may be impossible to win the belief on every element of the criteria. When this happens, a better syllogism is:

Any system in which the advantages outweigh the disadvantages should not be condemned.

This system is one in which the advantages outweigh the disadvantages.

Therefore, this system should not be condemned.

This wording should be considered suggestive and you must adapt it to the particular situation at hand. The basis of it is merely to suggest to the audience that the majority of advantages, elements of the criteria, or truth is in favor of your advocacy. (The word system is used in the widest possible meaning. Depending on your argument, you can substitute such words as *person, place, institution, policy,* and so on.)

Proposition of Policy

In this type of proposition the main issues become premises on which the conclusion is based. Each evil attributed to the present system becomes a premise on which the conclusion—that there is a need for a change—is drawn. The benefits of the proposed new policy become the premises for the conclusion that it should be adopted. Thus the syllogism on which the proposition is based approximates the following:

Any policy that is an improvement over the present and is sufficiently free from new and greater objections should be adopted.

This policy is an improvement over the present and is sufficiently free from new and greater objections.

Therefore, this policy should be adopted.

In its simplest form, the establishment of a proposition of policy is based on comparison and contrast of the new policy with the old. Opponents of the new policy may turn to disjunctive deduction by suggesting alternatives other than the old policy and the one proposed. You must be ready to meet such arguments. They may suggest that the old policy could be modified or repaired; they could suggest alternative new solutions. The following syllogism suggests the basis for the discussion:

Either we retain the old policy or adopt the proposed one.

We must not retain the old.

Therefore, we should adopt the proposed policy.

You will use this kind of deduction more than any other; the various rules of deduction apply whenever it is used. Its weaknesses and its strengths should be utilized whether you are arguing for or against propositions.

In building your speeches, make sure you have violated as few of the tests for good deduction as possible or, if you are an advocate against a proposition, by the same means you will be able to defeat a proposal.

Summary of Lines of Argument on Deduction

For an advocate using categorical deduction:

1. The major premise is true or has been proved true.

2. The minor premise is true or has been proved true.

3. The specific case falls within (or probably falls within) the general rule. (The terms have been properly distributed.)

4. No double meaning is present among the terms of the argument. (There are only three terms.)

5. The conclusion has been drawn from positive, not negative, premises.

For evaluating or refuting categorical deduction:

1. The major premise is false or unproved.

2. The minor premise is false or unproved.

3. In lack of distribution of terms

    a. The specific case can be an exception to the general rule.

    b. The specific case is true of only some, not all.

    c. The speaker has not demonstrated that the members of the group mentioned are the only ones.

4. When four terms are used

    a. The argument has been built on premises that are unrelated.

    b. The argument has been built on equivocation, or double meaning.

5. The conclusion has been drawn from unrelated or negative premises.

For an advocate using disjunctive deduction:

1. The major premise is true or has been proved true.

2. The major premise contains all possible alternatives.

3. The alternatives stated are mutually exclusive.

4. The minor premise is true or has been proved true.

5. Other forms of reasoning and evidence support the conclusion.

For evaluating or refuting disjunctive deduction:

1. The major premise is false or unproved.

2. There are additional alternatives.

3. The alternatives are not mutually exclusive.

4. The minor premise is false.

5 Other forms of reasoning and evidence prove the conclusion false.

For an advocate using hypothetical deduction:

1. The major premise is true or has been proved true.

2. The minor premise is true or has been proved true.

3. If using causal lines of argument, be sure to have tested with the rules of hypothetical deduction.

For evaluating or refuting hypothetical deduction:

1. The major premise is false or unproved.

2. The minor premise is false or unproved.

3. After applying the tests of hypothetical deduction to find possible fallacy, utilize causal lines of argument.

EXERCISES

1. Define:

   a. Deductive reasoning

   b. A syllogism

   c. A major premise

   d. A minor premise

   e. A major term

   f. A minor term

   g. A middle term

   h. Enthymeme

   i. Categorical deduction

   j. Disjunctive deduction

   k. Hypothetical deduction

   l. Sorites

   m. Equivocation

   n. A conditional clause

   o. Antecedent

   p. Consequent

2. With what kinds of propositions is deduction effective?

3. In what way is deductive reasoning closely related to the establishment of the main issues of a proposition?

4. Just how is deduction involved in proving that a particular thing is harmful?

5. Why is it valuable to develop your skill in changing enthymemes into syllogisms?

6. Change the following enthymemes into syllogisms:

a. This system has four serious evils; it should be abolished.

b. Government censorship of movies will threaten freedom of expression; it should never be adopted.

c. Since she is from Hong Kong, she must be able to speak Chinese.

d. Our star forward can play tonight; therefore we will win.

e. Our opponents cannot win tonight; therefore we will.

f. I am sure he speaks French, he is from Paris.

g. Speech codes for professors could destroy academic freedom; therefore they should be avoided.

h. Since she is from Massachusetts, she must be a Democrat.

i. After all, all humans make mistakes and she is a human.

j. Our traditional rival won't win the championship; therefore our college will.

k. Most people who live in Vermont are liberals; therefore your cousin must be.

l. The Green Party can't win the next election; therefore the Democrats will.

m. She knows how to use arguments effectively; thus she can win their belief.

n. This system has three advantages; therefore it should be retained.

o. People from the South are more relaxed and she is from the South.

7. The following are attempts at deductive reasoning. Explain why each is deductive in nature and use one or more lines of argument to evaluate or refute it.

a. John Brown must be a member of the Animal Liberation Front. He believes it morally right to destroy private property to protect animal rights.

b. Alcoholism is a dreaded disease; drinking is the cause of alcoholism; therefore, drinking leads to this dreaded disease.

c. Pine wood is good for lumber; matches are pine wood; therefore matches are good for lumber.

d. She is not unemployed; therefore she must be a working person.

e. It is obvious that Sarah Vinez is a terrorist; she is a member of two organizations that have been listed as terrorist groups by the U.S. Federal Bureau of Investigation.

f. She will frown on drinking at our faculty party; she is the dean of students.

g. Most people agree that it has been good for labor to unionize; then why shouldn't professors unionize? After all, they have to labor for a living.

h. Of course Jim Johnson believes in national health insurance; he has stated again and again that he is a Democrat.

i. Ira Simpson must be interested in athletics; he is a college student.

j. Most people agree that it is good for a person to develop social relationships. Then why shouldn't all students join a fraternity or sorority? After all, fraternities and sororities are chiefly concerned with social life.

k. Since the United Nations can't accomplish its basic purpose of preventing war, it should be abolished.

l. Since she works at the Ford plant, she must be a member of a labor union.

m. The profit motive has brought us greed and more greed; therefore we should replace it with a more socially responsible motive.

Chapter 8
Influencing Through Causal Reasoning

The more we know of the world about us, the more we observe relationships among events. Spring rains and warmer weather cause the grass to grow. Germs can bring diseases. Broken homes often bring juvenile delinquency. Certain events, therefore, become causal forces to bring about other events. Knowing this, people have set out to control the world in which they live. The introduction of new types of medical treatment has reduced the number and extent of epidemics in the world. Boys' clubs, girls' organizations, and the construction of recreational facilities are supposed to prevent juvenile delinquency. Fines and imprisonment are used to deter would be criminals. People use these kinds of forces to control the world in which they live.

PROPOSITIONS WITH WHICH CAUSAL REASONING IS EFFECTIVE

Much of your time as a speaker will be used in talking about various factors of control. You will be talking about the causal forces that humankind has used to control society, about the changes that are needed, or about the introduction of new causal forces that are required to improve conditions. Several propositions will require causal reasoning to develop. You use causal reasoning to develop the proposition that the policies of the present system cause certain evils that demand a change. If you are defending the present system, you will speak on the proposition that the policies of the present system have advantages. Whenever you introduce a new solution, you will use causal reasoning to show that your proposed new solution will remove the evils existing in the present system. You may strengthen your argument further by suggesting that the solution not only will remove those evils but also will bring additional benefits. On the other hand, if you are opposing the introduction of some new scheme or solution, you will use causal reasoning to develop the proposition that new and dangerous objections will arise should the new system be adopted. Whenever you are developing a problem solution speech, causal reasoning may be the basic kind of argument that you will be using.

CAUSAL REASONING DEFINED

Causal reasoning is that form of reasoning in which an individual demonstrates that an event that happens first has the means, power, facilities, and/or desire to produce a second event. We often suggest to a friend, "You'll get wet because it is raining." In this case, we are suggesting a certain conclusion, namely, that the person will get wet. This is our proposition to be proved. Our support or proof for the proposition is the statement that it is raining. Or, again, we may argue, "You have the measles, you must have caught them from Simon; you were playing cards with him the day he was becoming sick with the measles." The actual process of causal reasoning in its simplest form is merely the statement of either a cause or an event as sufficient support for the whole reasoning process. This was true in the first case where the individual cited rain as the obvious reason why one would get wet. In most of your speaking, however, your causal reasoning will take the form of explaining why the cause produces the means, the power, the facilities, and/or the desire to result in the effect suggested. For example, if you are an advocate of guaranteed annual minimum income, and you are trying to develop the proposition that incomes will bring greater security for citizens, you would point out why this will be the case.

The process of causal reasoning can be explained by the following diagram:

Event 1 > Event 2

The causal reasoning you will use will be in the form of a theoretical explanation of the powerful forces represented by the arrow in the diagram. The more obvious and reasonable your explanation appears, the stronger your impact will be on your listener.

Causal reasoning is the process of giving that theoretical explanation. However, you may substantiate causal relationships by other forms of support or reasoning. After giving the theoretical explanation, you can cite authorities that attest to the existence of that causal relationship. You may refer to experts in the field who will cite the same forces at work that you yourself have suggested. You need not stop there, however; causal relationships can be established by induction as well. To prove that flossing would reduce tooth decay, you state that flossing was done by thousands of people in one study; it was then used in a second study, and in a third. As each of the three experiments brought the same results in thousands of cases, you can say that the causal relationship was fairly well proved. Thus, by definition, causal reasoning is actually the theoretical explanation of the forces that make it possible for event one, the cause, to produce or bring about event two, the effect. Remember that your argument may be made more convincing by utilizing additional forms of reasoning to strengthen the beliefs in the causal relationships.

TYPES OF CAUSAL REASONING

You as a speaker should know of and be capable of using the four different types of causal reasoning.

Cause-to-Effect Reasoning

This form of causal reasoning cites a known cause to prove that a specific effect did or will follow. Consider this example: "She is studying hard; therefore she will make good grades." We are trying to prove the effect, "she will make good grades." We do this by citing the known cause, "studying hard." Or again we may cite the cause, "It has been hot the last five days," and conclude, "therefore it will be warm enough for swimming." The cause, hot weather, has been used to prove the effect of being warm enough to swim.

Known Cause > Effect (to be proved)

The above diagram illustrates that a speaker may cite a cause and then draw the conclusion with reference to the effect. On the other hand, the effect may be stated as something to be proved and then the speaker proceeds to cite the cause as the proof for the effect: "I know I am more logical; I have taken a course in argumentation."

Effect-to-Cause Reasoning

This second type of causal reasoning is exactly opposite of the one just described. Effect-to-cause reasoning is that form of causal reasoning in which a known effect is cited to prove a cause. A common form of this reasoning is,

"She is all wet; it must be raining outside." The observable effect that she is wet is used as proof for the cause, "It is raining outside." The Great Depression of the 1930s had many known and observable effects. In the United States some 15 million people were unemployed; many banks were failing; most businesses were operating in deficit. These were obvious effects. We reasoned from them to their causes. We reasoned that we had overproduction, that we had extended credit too far, that we had overcapitalized our economy. All these were causes that we tried to prove by citing the effects. The last two world wars have had the known effects of many millions dead, many others wounded, and great destruction of homes and property. From these we tried to argue back that certain causes were operating to produce those wars. This type of reasoning can be diagramed as follows:

Known or Observed Effect > Cause to Be Proved

Notice that the reasoning is the reverse of that in cause-to-effect reasoning. The effect is known and we use it to prove the unknown cause.

A word of warning. Don't let the sequence of citation confuse you. In this effect-to-cause reasoning, the effect can be cited first to prove the unknown cause that is cited second. Alternatively, you can first cite the unknown cause that is to be proved by the known effect that you cite second. You can ask two questions to determine whether you are dealing with cause-to-effect or effect-to-cause reasoning. First, you can ask yourself, "Which is known, the effect or the cause?" If the effect is known, and is factual, then it must be effect-to-cause reasoning. If the cause is known and factual, then it must be cause-to-effect reasoning. Or you can ask yourself, "Which is being used to prove the other? Is a known cause being used to prove an effect?" If so, it is cause-to-effect reasoning. If a known effect is being used to prove a cause, then it is effect-to-cause reasoning.

Effect-to-Effect Reasoning

The third type of causal reasoning uses one effect to prove another effect. This proof is achieved on the basis that both effects have either a common or a similar cause. Our selections of books to read are often made by this type of reasoning. We read a good book (effect) and note the author (cause); we then select another of that author's books to read (effect). We see a good movie, note either its director or star, and then proceed to see the next one involving that director or star. We see some system bringing good effects to some other city or locality; on those grounds we advocate its adoption in our own city or locality. This too is effect-to-effect reasoning.

Argument from Sign Reasoning

Argument from sign is that form of causal reasoning that demonstrates that the presence of one event reveals the presence of a second event, there being an indirect or circuitous causal relationship existing between the two events. For example, suppose we are driving down a road and pass a school sometime during the months of September through May; we observe that a flag is flying and reason that school is in session. The flag flying in the schoolyard is a sign that the school is in operation. The events of school in session and the flag flying have a causal relationship that exists between them that is indirect. The direct and immediate cause of the flag flying may be that a janitor, little Johnny, or even a teacher took the flag out that morning and raised it. "School in session" was not the direct causal force of raising the flag. Despite the circuitous or indirect reasoning, the conclusion that school is in progress is a fairly sound one. Consider another example. The struggle over civil rights legislation in the United States in the 1960s, the turmoil in the South requiring governors of southern states to call out the militia or the National Guard to preserve order in towns where desegregation was taking place, were all signs of the unrest of the South over the race problem. The increase in juvenile crime, the increase in broken homes, the increase in the use of narcotics, the increase in the number of babies born out of wedlock are all signs of the problems that arose from post–World War II prosperity. All of these signs or symptoms could be called the effects arising from some cause. The causes in back of these signs are complex and numerous; in many cases they are distinctly indirect. Of importance here is to note that the sign tends to be an effect of a cause or causes that are indirect or circuitous. Thus, in the definition referred to above, Event One is an effect that is called a "sign" for Event Two, which is a cause that is rather indirect or circuitous in its relationship to that effect.

Causal Lines of Argument

As with all types of reasoning, certain lines of argument become quite effective in establishing causal relationships or in evaluating or refuting the causal reasoning of others. For you to use causal reasoning effectively as an advocate, you should learn each of these lines of argument and have them available on the tip of your tongue in any case where causal reasoning is being used.

Does the Alleged Cause Have the Means, Power, Facilities, and/or Desire to Produce the Effect?

This first line of argument on causal reasoning is one of the strongest and one that you should understand very clearly. The particular wording was used by Aristotle in his *Rhetoric* to explain the argument of probability. He pointed out that if a person had the means, the power, the facilities, and the desire to do something, he would do it unless checked by some counter cause. These four words should indicate to you some of the words that might be used in debate. You can substitute others. One could substitute the word *money* for the word *means*, the term *legal authority* for the word *power*, the word *machinery* for the word *facilities*. What words you use should depend on the subject you are discussing. Essentially, the question is, does the alleged cause have the force within it to produce the alleged effect. In a court trial for murder, the prosecutor will have the strongest possible case if she shows that the alleged murderer is an individual who had the strongest of motives, that he was present in the neighborhood of the crime, that he had the weapon available. The defense attorney, on the other hand, could weaken the stand of the prosecutor by showing the absence of desire on the part of the defendant to murder the victim. Thus, in those cases where you are building a causal argument, such as in advocating a new solution to a problem, your argument will be extremely powerful if you show that your solution has available the means, the power, and all the facilities and machinery necessary to achieve the result; and furthermore that your solution will increase the desire to actually remove the evil. If you are evaluating or refuting an argument of this type, you need only point out that one of these conditions is lacking. If two or more are lacking, then you weaken the argument of the advocate that much more.

Is This the Sole Cause or Are There Other Causes?

If an advocate, in analyzing the causal forces within the subject with which he is dealing, can single out one particular cause, he is fortunate. He has only one causal force to deal with, so that his job of convincing the audience will be simpler. Scarlet fever is caused by one type of germ. Accordingly, medical researchers more easily isolated the causal bacteria and discovered the best way to treat the disease. On the other hand, mental illness seldom, if ever, has a single or sole cause. An advocate who finds herself in the position of having a single cause in her proposition can suggest that cause to the audience and thereby simplify her task and strengthen her argument. On the other hand, to evaluate or refute causal reasoning, pointing out that the cause suggested by the advocate cannot be the sole cause because other causes are operating is frequently an effective tactic. You should then go on to point out other causes. In doing so, you may want to cite as many causes as you can to create the impression that the single cause suggested by the advocate is weak, or you may cite fewer causes but point out the great strengths of those causes that you do cite. Let us presume for a moment that you are confronted with a speaker who seems to imply that the sole cause of the Great Depression of the 1930s was greed. You could evaluate or refute this speaker by suggesting such other causes as the depressions in other nations that brought about a decline in our exports, the flooding of domestic markets with the repossessed articles of the unemployed, and the inability of management to predict completely the changing desires and real demand of the buying public. Thus, if you are an advocate and you have a chance to indicate that there is a sole cause, it strengthens your argument. If you are an evaluator or a refuter and desire to weaken the argument of a sole-cause advocate, then you can point to the existence of other causes.

Is This Cause Significant or Insignificant?

The significant cause argument is available to you as speaker and is a powerful tool in a world in which innumerable causes operate in so many areas. Instead of trying to suggest or even imply that the cause you are talking about is the sole cause, you may qualify by merely suggesting that it is one of the significant causes operating in the situation. You suggest that it is significant on the grounds that associated with it are the strong means, power, and facilities to bring about the observed effects. The "significant cause" line of argument is effective because the speaker seems to be understating her case rather than overstating it. The advocate suggesting that greed is a causal force in depressions strengthens her argument by suggesting that greed is a significant force operating to make depressions worse. To say to an audience that greed is the only cause of all depressions seems an overstatement; members of the audience will be thinking of other causes that may play a part in which greed does not seem to be present.

The evaluator or refuter can use the opposite line of reasoning. He can suggest that the cause cited is insignificant, that it is trivial. The evaluator or refuter will develop this line of argument on the basis of the lack of means, power, facility, or desire—the cause suggested does not have the force to produce any strong effect, particularly the effect cited. For example, those who advocated the recognition of "pariah" nations frequently made the argument that recognition with ensuing negotiations could settle disputes. Those against recognition used the "insignificant cause" line of argument by showing that negotiations will hardly deter totalitarian "pariah" countries from doing whatever they desire.

Is This an Original or Contributing Cause?

The planting of corn in the field may be the original cause for that crop being in that field. The contributing causes, however, of fertile soil and proper weather have a lot to do with the quality and quantity of the resulting crop. The good speaker is careful to discern whether the cause he is citing is original cause or what should be called only a contributing cause. You will make many propositions in which you will use the original cause and the contributing cause lines of argument. In arguments on subjects dealing with international relations, such original causes as dictators' lust for power or the desire of nations lacking raw materials to acquire them will frequently be heard. Conferences, negotiations, and conciliation will usually be cited as merely contributory causes to the peaceful settlements of disputes; it might even be suggested that a strong armed force is a contributory cause for peace.

In propositions of policy you as speaker will advocate that a new policy or a new solution be adopted. In the first part of your speech, you will have demonstrated that the present system or a present or existing policy is bad and pointed out the cause. In the second part of your speech, you will advocate a new policy or a new solution to overcome the shortcomings of the present policy or system. In pleading your case for the new policy or solution, if you can show that your new solution will remove the original cause of the problem you will have a strong solution. In other words, any solution that eliminates the original cause of a problem tends to be superior one. Penicillin is a remedy to get rid of the original cause of some diseases; it is used to kill the germs that caused the diseases. Several U.S. presidents won office although they did not win the popular vote. The original cause is the Electoral College. Those advocating the abolishment of the Electoral College are advocating a solution that is intended to rid us of the original cause of the problem. In most cases, the advocate who is able to demonstrate that she is removing the original causes of a problem has a stronger chance of persuasion; her solution seems a better one. Thus, if your proposed solution can reduce or modify the original cause of the problem, it is stronger than if it is merely a solution offering a contributory cause or causes. The evaluator, or refuter, on the other hand, should be quick to point out the original cause of a problem and, when only a contributory-cause solution is offered, suggest the weakness of such an argument. Those opposed to the recognition of "pariah" nations are quick to point out that at best recognition could only be a contributory cause to the reduction of tensions between the democracies and these countries, not a proposal that would remove the original cause of those tensions.

Are There or Will There Be Counteracting Causes?

Let us note again that Aristotle in his *Rhetoric* suggested that if a person had the means, the facilities, the power, and the desire to do something, he would proceed unless some counteracting cause entered the picture. A counteracting cause is any incident or force that will prevent events from occurring. Laws with penalties attached are counteracting forces by which society attempts to control humankind. The likelihood of getting caught and the death penalty become counteracting forces to prevent kidnapping. Fines and the suspension of licenses become counteracting forces against reckless driving. The solutions established for many problems could be called "counteracting-cause" solutions. Whenever you are advocating a certain solution to a problem be aware of whether you are advocating a counter-cause solution or one that is a substitution of a new cause for an old one. The more critical your audience, the more essential is this discrimination to success. Immediately counter the objection that you are doing nothing to remove the original cause and leave the impression of accurately evaluating the solution rather than overstating the case. On the other hand, whenever you are advocating a new policy or course of action, you may sometimes enhance your position by suggesting that no serious counteracting causal forces will arise. In this case you are picturing the probability of the solution working. Be careful not to use this line too often as you may suggest to your listeners aspects of the problem or proposed solution that had not occurred to them. On the other hand, this latter line of argument is quite effective when these counteracting forces have been widely predicted.

The evaluator or refuter will find the counteracting cause line of argument a very strong weapon through picturing to the audience the counteracting forces that may arise. A law may fail because too few are available to enforce it; a heavy penalty may fail because the courts may be reluctant to impose it;

a worthy project may never be initiated because it lacks widespread public financial support. The United States thought it could legislate away the evils of alcohol by a federal law; however, the counteracting cause of lack of widespread public approval led to the failure of Prohibition. Whenever you oppose the adoption of a certain policy, be sure to build numerous counter cause lines of argument—quantity as well as quality may overwhelm and defeat. The great speaker not only discovers the various counter causes that may operate as suggested by the authorities but also uses her imagination to predict others.

Has Coincidence Been Mistaken for Causal Relationship?

Because the mistaking of coincidence for causal relationship is fallacious, this kind of argument is limited to the person who is evaluating or refuting an argument. At most an advocate could merely suggest, "This is not coincidence." This fallacy occurs when Event Two follows Event One in a fashion similar to the events in causal relationships, causing individuals to assume a connection that does not exist between the two events. Thus superstitions have arisen and people have attested to their truth. Plenty of people have had bad luck on Friday the 13th or after black cats have run across their paths or after breaking mirrors. To demonstrate this as coincidence should be relatively easy if you have an educated audience. You can demonstrate that the act of a cat running across our path has no particular means, facilities, power, or desire to influence our lives in any way. You can picture for the audience that the only causal force operating in this case is our fear bred by the superstition. In other cases, the picturing of the coincidence is more difficult. In the following cases, for instance, is the event pure coincidence or is a causal relationship present? Event One—education in the United States has increased; Event Two—crime has increased; therefore, the increase in education has caused an increase in crime. Or, Event One—the standard of living in the United States has increased; Event Two—crime has increased; therefore, the increase in the standard of living causes an increase in crime.

In addition to using the first line of argument (means, power, facilities and/or desire), you may also use the line of argument that demonstrates how frequently Event One has happened without Event Two or vice versa. The technique in using this line of argument is to accuse the individual you are evaluating or refuting of having mistaken coincidence for causal relationship and then to use additional lines of argument to further substantiate your contention for your audience.

Summary of Lines of Argument on Causal Reasoning

1. The suggested cause has the means, power, facilities, and/or desire to produce the effect.

2. This is the sole cause; no other causes were operating.

3. Among the causes operating, one is very significant.

4. Both original and contributing causes are important in this world; controlling, modifying, reducing will effect a significant change.

5. This will be an important counteracting cause helping to reduce the problem.

To Evaluate or Refute Causal Reasoning

1. The alleged cause lacks the means, power, facilities, and/or desire to produce the suggested effect.

2. This cannot be the sole cause because of the operation of the following specific causes.

3. The alleged cause is quite insignificant.

4. The speaker is ignoring the original cause; at best she is only speaking of a contributing cause.

5. The following counteracting causes have been or will be operating.

6. The gentleperson has mistaken coincidence for causal relationship.

Exercises

1. Define:

   a. Causal reasoning

   b. Cause-to-Effect reasoning

   c. Effect-to-Cause reasoning

   d. Effect-to-Effect reasoning

   e. Argument from sign

2. With what types of propositions is causal reasoning effective?

3. What is meant by "means, power, facilities"?

4. When does desire become a significant part of causal reasoning and when is it absent?

5. Motivation is an important factor in learning as well as in other endeavors. How is it related to desire? How significant is it in human behavior?

6. Define the following:

    a. Sole cause

    b. Other causes

    c. Significant cause

    d. Insignificant cause

    e. Original cause

    f. Contributing cause

    g. Counteracting cause

    h. Coincidence

7. The following are attempts at causal reasoning. Explain why the reasoning attempted is causal and use one or more lines of argument to evaluate or refute it:

    a. In the last 100 years we have improved the educational system and more people are getting better and better education. In those same years, however, the per capita crime rate has been increasing. One of the evils of education, despite all its great benefits, is that education does produce a higher crime rate.

    b. Obviously our laws against serving alcohol to minors do not carry severe enough penalties. Look at the great number of cases where alcoholic drinks are sold to them.

    c. I just broke a mirror; therefore I can expect to have bad luck.

    d. Children wouldn't commit murders if they knew they would be tried as adults.

    e. We must conclude that our laws controlling narcotics are not good. Otherwise we wouldn't have so many people using narcotics.

    f. Thirteen people sat down at the table to eat today; therefore we will have a misfortune soon.

    g. Crimes among immigrants have increased since they have been given better access to education. Therefore, the growth of crime among immigrants results from the greater educational level of immigrants.

h. She is all wet; it must be raining outside.

i. There wouldn't be so much reckless driving on our roads if our laws carried heavier penalties.

j. We must make sure that we do as much as possible to prevent murder; therefore we must never abolish capital punishment.

k. She is training for the race; obviously she will win it.

l. Leaving the cleaning up of stream pollution to local government units will never work. The local units are not cleaning up the water for themselves but for communities down the stream, thus they never have the incentive.

m. I have taken a course in argumentation. It must inevitably follow that I am now a more logical person.

Chapter 9
Influencing Through Reasoning from Analogy

Contrary to the opinions of some, the use of reasoning from analogy to influence the attitudes of others is effective. During our lives we are taught to profit from the experience of others. We have been told that history can teach us much, and we often ask how a course of action failed or succeeded in other places. These questions and admonitions are based on the effect of reasoning from analogy on us. All induction is based on factual examples that are sufficiently analogous to be meaningful. Teachers and impartial investigators, as well as advocates, are constantly drawing conclusions based on the experiences of others.

PROPOSITIONS WITH WHICH REASONING FROM ANALOGY IS EFFECTIVE

You, as an advocate, will use reasoning from analogy on a variety of propositions. You may use it to gain the belief that your new proposal will remove the evils or solve the problems of the present system. You may use the experiences of individuals in other places to show that your proposal can work successfully because it worked successfully elsewhere. By making a comparison with other places, you may show that your new proposal can be administered easily. On the other hand, you may try to turn opinion against a proposal by showing the impracticalities revealed by its use in other localities. Or again, you may use the experiences of others to show that a new proposal will generate dangerous objections otherwise unsuspected. Reasoning from analogy is used in the law court in the form of referring to other cases that set precedents that should be followed in the case on trial. These and many other propositions may be supported with reasoning from analogy.

Reasoning from Analogy Defined

Reasoning from analogy is that form of reasoning in which it is demonstrated that what occurred in one situation will occur in a similar situation. In its simplest form, we merely suggest to an audience that what happened there will happen here. The following is the diagram of this reasoning process:

It happened there > It will happen here

In using analogy, you must compare like things, which must be of the same class, such as people to people, horses to horses, pine trees to pine trees. Natural laws tend to operate in the same way, or at least in a similar way, among the similar classes of things. You must be careful to observe individual differences not only among people, but also among all categories of things; otherwise reasoning from analogy can be weak. So important are these individual differences that some people make the exaggerated claim that reasoning from analogy can never be sound. Accordingly, you must make sure that you are comparing like things, always keeping in mind that individual differences may weaken your comparison.

On the other hand, humankind has made vital discoveries by comparing things that seemed to be of differing classes. In the field of medicine, many of our new vaccines were tried on animals before being tried on human beings. Psychologists have learned much about human behavior by the study of rats; Pavlov experimented on a dog to discover many of the features of the conditioned reflex. In these cases, the similarities were so great that significant discoveries were made. Thus, reasoning from analogy can be strong, as witnessed by the fact that it has helped us uncover much knowledge in the past.

In this chapter we are considering reasoning from literal, rather than figurative, analogy. No sound conclusion can be drawn from figurative analogies; on the other hand, reasoning with literal analogy has its merits. Literal analogy compares like things such as cities to cities, geographic places to geographic places. Figurative analogy compares unlike things such as the heart of the human body with the heart of a city or the heart of government. Figurative analogy has the power to explain and the power to arouse emotions; literal analogy, comparing things of a like nature, often has the power of logic behind it.

RELATIONSHIP TO INDUCTION

Reasoning from analogy is so closely related to reasoning from induction—both are based on factual examples—that some writers in the field of argumentation place their discussion of both forms of reasoning under the same chapter title: "reasoning from examples." If we investigate Eugene, Oregon, as a place where community ownership and operation of electricity has worked successfully, and then conclude that a similar-size town such as Ann Arbor, Michigan, would have the same experience, we are reasoning from a factual example—that is reasoning from analogy. On the other hand, we may make a survey of many of the cities that have community ownership and operation of electric plants and draw the conclusion that such operations are successful; when we do this we will be using a sufficient number of factual examples to prove the generalization.

The most prominent fallacy in reasoning from analogy is the attempt to compare dissimilar cases. Induction based on examples that are not analogous (not comparable) is likewise fallacious. We remind you here of the line of argument under evidence: "Are the statistical units sufficiently comparable?" In general, reasoning from induction will be stronger than reasoning from analogy because induction uses many examples, while reasoning from analogy uses at most two or three examples and often depends on only one. When reasoning from induction using many examples, you may make use of the bell-curve spread, citing from the many cities, for example, that have had great, moderate, and not so great success with community ownership of power plants. You would be substantiating your argument by showing that some success has been achieved in all cases. Reasoning from analogy is useful in supporting propositions when a policy has been tried only in a few cases—so few that induction is impossible.

RELATIONSHIP TO CAUSAL REASONING

Most, if not all, of your use of reasoning from analogy will be effect-to-effect reasoning. The above example of community operation of electric plants by cities uses effect-to-effect reasoning. The cause, community ownership and operation, had the effect in Eugene of producing electricity at a cost that satisfied residents. Your argument would be that the introduction of the same cause in other cities that are sufficiently similar will produce the same effect. The result is that when you use reasoning from analogy you may find yourself engaged in the causal relationship analysis of both the factual example you are using to prove your case and the causal forces in operation in the new locality. Thus, the lines of argument available on causal reasoning will be applicable to those examples cited in reasoning from analogy. In other words, you would study the effects of community ownership of electricity in Eugene rather thoroughly to find out whether the effects are good or bad.

On the other hand, reasoning from analogy may often constitute the factual proof for causal reasoning. Not only do you establish causal reasoning by showing that the alleged cause has the means, power, facilities, and/or desire to produce the effect, you may also cite a single factual example to prove that your assertion is true. When you do, you are using the essential features of reasoning from analogy.

LINES OF ARGUMENT FOR REASONING FROM ANALOGY

The following are those lines of argument most frequently used in connection with reasoning from analogy:

Do the Similarities Outweigh the Differences?

In using this line of argument, you picture for your audience the great number of similarities between the two examples cited. If the analogy is between countries, you cite similarities of government, educational level of the people, population, economic systems, and the like. In comparing two periods of history, you cite as many economic, political, social, cultural, and educational similarities as possible. The effective use of this line of argument will depend on the speaker's ability to analyze the significant factors in the two situations that he is trying to compare.

Do the Differences Outweigh the Similarities?

This line of argument is for the individual who wants to refute or evaluate the analogies used by others. The speaker should list all the things that differ in the two situations—differences in forms of government, population, cultures of the people, and economic systems. She should particularly show that the people were facing a distinctly different set of problems. In this quantitative type of argument, great numbers of differences will impress the audience.

Are the Similarities or Differences Significant or Insignificant?

Your procedure will depend on whether you are arguing for or against the particular analogy. To strengthen the argument for the analogy, you may suggest that only likenesses that are significant to the argument should be considered. In doing so, you will maximize those similarities that are most pertinent to your comparison and minimize those dissimilarities that seem more likely to be irrelevant. For example, should you choose to compare the United States with the United Kingdom, you would maximize the similarities of government, level of education, common cultural heritages, and high standard of industrial development. You would minimize such dissimilarities as size of population, geographical location, and access to raw materials.

In refutation or evaluation the significant dissimilarities are emphasized. The individual evaluating or refuting the comparison between ownership and operation of electric power in Eugene, Oregon, and Ann Arbor, Michigan, would minimize the similarities—the size of the two towns, both being homes of state universities, and that both had similar forms of government; she would maximize the significant difference in geography. The city of Eugene is close to both the Willamette and MacKenzie rivers that drain thousands of acres of the Cascade Mountain Range and thus is in the happy position of being able to develop hydroelectric power. The consequence? Charges for electric power in Eugene ought to be drastically different from those of Ann Arbor, which lies in the flat lands of the Midwest. You should become adept when using reasoning from analogy in selecting those particular factors that are significant similarities or significant dissimilarities.

The foregoing are the lines of argument specific to reasoning from analogy. Available to you in establishing or refuting analogy are lines of argument on causal reasoning and the lines of argument on evidence. Because reasoning from analogy is really reasoning from effect-to-effect, causal lines of argument will readily apply in many cases. Because reasoning from literal analogy is factual, the lines of argument on evidence will apply. Facts must be substantiated by reliable authorities whose observation can be trusted because they are trained in research, free from prejudice, and have actually made a study.

Summary of Lines of Argument by Analogy

1. The similarities between the two examples cited outweigh the differences.

2. The differences between the two examples cited outweigh the similarities.

3. The significant similarities outweigh the differences, which are insignificant.

4. The significant differences outweigh the similarities, which are insignificant.

Summary of the Interrelationships of the Various Types of Reasoning

In Chapters 6, 7, 8, and 9, we have discussed the various types of reasoning and the lines of argument connected with each. Before we leave the subject, we want to take note of the strong interrelationships among the various types of reasoning. As with most other college subjects, we may categorize the various parts of the subject, but however essential for study, this separation into parts seldom exists in reality. In logic, the various forms are so interrelated that one depends on the other. We can begin with any one of them and go around the circle and find several relationships. We have already noted that reasoning from analogy is related to induction—various examples within induction must be analogous for the generalization to be made. Induction, on the other hand, is used both to prove that a causal relationship exists and to establish premises on which deduction is built. As indicated earlier, the premise (the fact) that "all humans die" was established by inductive reasoning. On the other hand, deduction must be added to induction to form a conclusion about that fact. Not only must we prove inductively that all humans die, but by deduction, we must show this is good or bad. Often we will combine induction with deduction to predict the future. We inductively prove that a certain generalization was true through many past experiences, then draw the conclusion that, therefore, the future will see this happen again. Causal relationships, on the other hand, are often established by induction or else exist within the premises of deduction.

These are many of the relationships that you may have already noted about the various forms of reasoning. Because of these interrelationships among the various forms of reasoning, some people have difficulty identifying the particular type being used at the moment. The clue to identification of the type of reasoning is the process being used. Is the process one of drawing a generalized conclusion from a number of specific examples? If so, then the speaker is attempting to reason inductively. Is the speaker merely suggesting that a specific occurrence happened in that place, therefore it will happen in this? If so, then the process is that of reasoning from analogy. If the speaker is trying to show that a certain event has the power to bring about a second event, the speaker is using causal reasoning. Finally, if the process uses premises to arrive at a conclusion, the process is deduction.

To help you evaluate or refute an argument, to see whether or not it is worthy of belief, begin by identifying the type of reasoning attempted and then start with the lines of argument in that field. However, sometimes the greatest weaknesses of the argument can be revealed by turning to lines of argument related to other types of reasoning.

EXERCISES

1. Define:

   a. Reasoning from analogy

   b. Literal analogy

   c. Figurative analogy

2. With what kinds of proposition is reasoning from analogy effective?

3. What is the relationship between induction and reasoning from analogy?

4. Why is the line of argument on statistics, "Are the units comparable?" related to reasoning from analogy?

5. Why can it be said that figurative analogy has no basis in logic?

6. How are causal reasoning and reasoning from analogy related?

7. The following are attempts at reasoning from analogy. Explain why the reasoning attempted is analogous and use one or more lines of argument to evaluate or refute.

   a. After Great Britain recognized Cuba, anti-British propaganda decreased. If the United States should recognize Cuba, we could expect a decrease in anti-American propaganda.

   b. After Great Britain adopted national health insurance, the life expectancy of its citizens increased. Were the United States to adopt national health insurance, we could also expect such an increase in life expectancy.

   c. Our city would have a more efficient form of government if a city manager system were adopted. Every department of city government in Cincinnati became more efficient after adoption of the city manager system.

d. Michigan, which doesn't have capital punishment, has no more murders per capita than the average in other states. We can conclude that abolishing capital punishment in our state won't bring a higher murder rate.

e. Today in the United States, only a little more than half the eligible voters cast their ballots. In Belgium, with a compulsory voting law, 95 percent cast their ballots. To get a high percentage of our citizens to vote, we should pass a compulsory voting law.

f. Legalizing gambling will reduce police corruption. France and England both have legalized gambling and the amount of police corruption is about one half that of ours.

Chapter 10
Refutation: Blocking the Arguments of Others

On many occasions you will want to block the effectiveness of particular arguments. You will desire to have people follow a different policy from the one that is being advocated. When you do, you will need to be effective in the use of refutation.

DEFINITION

Refutation is that process of communication in which an individual directly attacks the arguments of others in an attempt to reduce the effectiveness and influence of those arguments on audiences. Refutation is employed in courtroom trials both by the defense attorney, who uses it to weaken the arguments that could convict her client, and by the prosecuting attorney, who must refute any new arguments brought into the trial by the defense attorney and also be prepared to counter-refute the refutation of the defense attorney. In legislatures, those who are opposed to the passage of bills will use refutation to try to weaken the arguments for their passage. Those in favor of such bills will refute any of the opposition's arguments and will also counter-refute the refutation to their own. Refutation will be in the air whenever differences of opinion arise and individuals become strong advocates of their own points of view.

In this chapter we will explain the various techniques of refutation. In going through the various forms of reasoning we have already uncovered many such techniques. In such cases we shall merely enumerate these devices again.

Refutation by Challenging Analysis and Definition

One of the first actions to take in refuting the advocacy of another is to challenge the definition of the terms of the proposition. If you can suggest to your audience that the individual advocating a certain policy doesn't understand that policy, hasn't interpreted it correctly, or is misleading the audience because of vague definitions, you will have struck a blow at the arguments. This is particularly true when you are able to uncover lack of knowledge on the part of an advocate about a new, long, and involved policy, such as laws passed by a government where the failure on the part of an advocate to know all these parts and to understand their implications weakens his advocacy of that new policy.

A problem that has confronted our governments from time to time has been the recognition of totalitarian nations. A person who advocates such recognition will often have trouble defining exactly such recognition. If she defines it as the meeting of representatives of the two nations to talk over problems, she will be at fault because such meetings have taken place without recognition. If she tries to use a specific historic example, she is liable to err, since the policy with reference to nonrecognition has changed from time to time. In pointing out these lacks, you can take a great stride toward weakening the arguments of such an advocate on the grounds that she doesn't know all the ramifications of her subject.

Equally, if not more, important is the challenging of analysis. You should constantly keep in view the overall structure of the arguments of the individual who holds an opposing point of view. Remember that he must prove each one of the main issues involved in his proposition. The prosecuting attorney may have demonstrated beautifully that the accused had plenty of motive, but if she fails to prove that the accused was in the vicinity where the crime took place, this should be pointed out quickly. Those advocating changes of policy may have built strong arguments on what is wrong with the present system but may be very weak or completely ignore the proof that the proposed solution can be put into effect or that it can remove the evils within the present system. You can also refute the analysis of another by suggesting that he has overlooked great dangers that are involved in the adoption of his proposal.

This fallacy of incomplete analysis has caused humankind many troubles and is likely to occur again and again. Incomplete analysis on the part of the administration of President George W. Bush led to a drawn out war in Iraq. The administration believed that Saddam Hussein had weapons of mass destruction, which were never found. Examples of weak or incomplete analysis abound throughout history. Alert yourself to every possibility of weakening the advocacy of others by suggesting fallacies in analysis or definition.

REFUTATION THROUGH MINIMIZING

An effective weapon of refutation is the process of minimizing the arguments of others. In minimizing arguments you do not deny the validity of the argument; the process is, rather, one in which you demonstrate quantitatively the minuscule worth of the arguments. Thus, you may readily admit that problems exist in our current systems but affirm that these problems aren't really very great. This may be done by suggesting that the worst and least typical examples or cases have been cited rather than the average ones. For example, you could refute any problems among single mothers by suggesting that the examples cited or that are noted in the newspapers are atypical and extreme. Another method of minimizing is to suggest that the evil is as widespread as is claimed but that quantitatively the harm is not so great. The "what harm" or "so what" argument is an effective tool for such minimizing. Minimizing has been the chief method of refutation by those who oppose any change in the Electoral College system of electing the president of the United States. The number of times a president has been elected against the popular will of the people has been too few to be significant.

The counter-refutation to minimizing is maximizing. If you have few examples, then you will need to emphasize the extreme harm or the extreme injustice in these few cases. Try to find additional examples of the problem or evil; they will greatly benefit your argument. Research and more research is of great importance to find such examples.

REFUTATION BY DENYING THE EVIDENCE

This method of refutation has the speaker attempting to undermine the evidence of the advocate. How? Merely apply any one or more of the nine lines of argument discussed in the chapter on evidence. They are as follows:

1. The authority has not made a study.

2. The authority quoted has not been trained in research.

3. The authority quoted is prejudiced.

4. The authority quoted is guilty of exaggeration.

5. The authority quoted is inconsistent in her beliefs.

Should the evidence be in the form of statistics, the following can also be used:

6. The statistical unit has not been defined.

7. The statistical units are not comparable.

8. Statistics are not an index to what we want to know; they are not an index to the conclusion of the speaker.

9. Other studies in the same area brought out different facts. (Cite the differing results of other studies.)

REFUTATION BY DEMONSTRATING THE OPPOSITE

This method of refutation, as the name implies, is one in which you deliberately show that the opposite conclusion should be drawn from that which the advocate suggests. The lines of argument "Other studies do not verify the conclusion" and "Negative instances show the contrary" are examples of this type of refutation. Frequently the method is more indirect and uses a deductive method. Where an advocate may be citing evils in the present system, you will show benefits or advantages of the present system. Where the advocate may be trying to show benefits of a new proposal, you in turn will show dangers or objections to the new proposal. Such methods as these are often used in the never ending debate over the advantages of various types of economic structures. Those who condemn twenty-first century capitalism point to the possibility of its encouraging greed and its stress on material achievement; they also point to the inequalities in income and wealth that it engenders. Others refute these points by discussing the advantages of capitalism, including the development of initiative, the profit derived from inventions, the creation of new ideas, and the progress capitalism has encouraged. They also point out the greater prestige received by and deference accorded to those who make a great deal of money. In propositions of fact, the refutation consists mainly in demonstrating the opposite. If a prosecuting attorney tries to show that the defendant was in the area of the crime, the defense attorney will often refute his case by proving the defendant was elsewhere. Showing that the number of unwanted pregnancies among teens has dramatically decreased in the last 15 years refutes those who maintain that the present system is failing to address the problem of unwanted pregnancies among teens.

Refutation by Exposing Fallacies in Reasoning

One of the more effective and more frequently used methods of refutation is that of exposing fallacies in reasoning. The fallacies in inductive, deductive, causal reasoning, and reasoning from analogy have been discussed in Chapters 6 through 9. The methods of exposing them have also been revealed and need no further discussion here. A summary of the fallacies in the form of lines of reasoning is included at the end of each chapter.

Refutation by Exposing Special Types of Fallacies

Certain types of fallacies are of such a nature that associating them with any type of reasoning is difficult. The processes involved are not inductive, deductive, causal, or reasoning from analogy. Often, however, you will gain an advantage by exposing these special types of fallacies should they occur in the reasoning process of some advocate whom you desire to refute.

Arguing in a Circle

Arguing in a circle occurs when two or more unproved propositions are used to establish each other. The following is an example of arguing in a circle: When guns are outlawed, only outlaws will have guns.

Difficulties often arise in revealing the existence of arguing in a circle. To make this fallacy clear, try rearranging the argument into two syllogisms. For example: Whatever is morally wrong should be prohibited; gay bashing is morally wrong, therefore gay bashing should be prohibited. The second syllogism would be: Whatever should be prohibited is morally wrong; gay bashing should be prohibited, therefore gay bashing is morally wrong. The absurdity of the second syllogism indicates the fallacy of circular reasoning..

Often the circular nature of the argument is not as clear as in this example because considerable discourse may take place between the argument's first part and its last. Discovering that the argument is circular often demands careful listening along with keen analysis.

Assuming a More General Truth that Involves the Point at Issue

This fallacy occurs when an individual tries to prove a more specific proposition by merely repeating that same proposition in a more generalized form. For example, "That fellow should have a heavy fine for not wearing a life preserver while waterskiing, for all such people should be heavily fined." The statement has an implied generalization; the fallacy arises from the fact that this generalization itself has not been proved. To expose this fallacy, turn again to the syllogistic form: Whoever water skis without a life preserver should be heavily fined. That fellow did not wear a life preserver. Therefore that fellow should be fined. Until the generalization that all people who water ski without a life preserver should be heavily fined is proved, the reasoning is fallacious.

The Fallacious Question

In the give and take of courtroom trials, in debate, or even in the daily discussion of problems, we frequently ask each other questions. A fallacious question is one that assumes the truth of things that really will have to be proved or to which either a yes or no answer will be damaging. A common example of this kind of question: "Have you stopped beating your wife?" This question is fallacious on both counts. First, it would have to be proved that the person was in the habit of beating his wife or had beaten her; second, it is fallacious because the responder is in the wrong whether he says "yes" or "no." To answer "yes" admits that he did beat his wife on occasion; if he answers "no," he then is admitting that he is still beating his wife. He just can't win.

You will run into fallacious questions many times in your life. Frequently they are asked to trip up the other person. The following are additional examples of fallacious questions:

    a. Are you more disinclined to believe in communism?

    b. Has your college stopped overemphasizing athletics?

    c. Did you write a long article in defense of the woman on trial?

The fallaciousness of the first two examples is rather obvious. The fallaciousness of the third becomes apparent by studying the possible meanings of a "no" answer. She might say "no" if she gave a speech instead of writing, if it were a short instead of a long article, or if it was not in defense of the woman. Only a qualified answer might be proper.

To expose this fallacy is to label the question as fallacious and to point out that the questioner is obligated to prove what is assumed to be true in the question or to point out that neither "yes" nor "no" answer is possible. You are perfectly justified in never answering such a question. In court trials the lawyers raise objections when such questions are asked and the judge determines that the witness need not answer.

Appeals to Prejudice (*Argumentum ad Populum*)

The word *prejudice*—meaning to judge with insufficient facts—comes from the prefix *pre* and the word *judge*, Sometimes a speaker will base her appeals on the known prejudices of the particular audience instead of logic; this is the fallacy of appealing to prejudice. Examples of appeals to prejudice are:

"This is what the people want."

"Public opinion polls reveal . . ."

"Everyone knows that Wall Street is trying to dominate the country."

Here the speaker is trying to depend on what is supposed to be the opinion of the public rather than trying to prove his case with logic. Appeals to prejudice are frequent and are often introduced with such phrases as: "We are the chosen few," "She is introducing a foreign idea," "They are unpatriotic." In all these cases the speaker is trying to base his appeal on our prejudices rather than on our powers of reasoning from evidence.

Your greatest chance to expose this fallacy will lie in the use of the lines of argument on evidence because the individual making the appeal to prejudice is trying to substitute the audience's prejudices for evidence. Frequently the lack of truth in such statements can be revealed by facts—no such study has ever been made, nobody has ever been able to uncover the facts cited, or that such a study would be completely impossible to do so. The old charge that Wall Street really controls the United States is exposed in such fashion: nobody has yet been able to prove that Wall Street is controlling the country—controlling it by deciding the votes of 100 senators and 435 representatives or controlling the votes of the various state legislators. At best, to show that Wall Street controls the country is difficult and lines of argument such as these may readily expose this fallacy.

Argument Involving Personalities (*Argumentum ad Hominem*)

Argument *ad hominem* means arguing "to the person," attacking the character of the individual or individuals who support a particular belief rather than addressing the evidence and argument that support the belief. The charge is made that only "fools, idiots, and misguided individuals would support such a belief." For example, "I am against privatizing social security because President George W. Bush is for it." The person condemned privatizing solely on the basis of who was for it rather than on the basis of a totality of the premises and evidence that would support the case for or against it. This argument is often pure name calling.

Various kinds of argument will help expose this particular fallacy. The most basic is simply to reveal that the speaker is guilty of this fallacy. Often, however, you can refute this fallacy by naming persons of great prestige who hold the same belief as the person attacked. In the long run, of course, this fallacy is best overcome by presenting a strong case supported by sound premises and good evidence to the contrary.

Shifting Ground

This fallacy occurs when an advocate discovers that a certain premise on which she is basing her argument is untenable and has to shift to another basis for her argument. She begins by presenting certain reasons for her ultimate conclusion, giving them up and turning to others when she finds her reasons unsupportable. We distinctly remember the occasion of a debate between two colleges on the subject: "The penalties for possessing marijuana should be increased." The affirmative team began by suggesting that marijuana was harmful. When the negative team provided excellent evidence that showed that penalties had no effect on the use of marijuana and thus its harms, the affirmative team shifted to grounds that society needed to make a strong moral stand against drugs. Again, the negative showed that marijuana had nothing immoral about it and that it was not a "drug" like cocaine or heroin. By that time the debate was too far gone for the affirmative to shift ground a third time.

The two chief causes of falling into this fallacy are lack of knowledge of the subject being discussed or exaggeration. Often advocates, in their desire to stimulate the audience, overstate their claims. When they do, the soundest refutation is to expose the exaggeration with well-authenticated facts, forcing a retreat from the original ground. Then the process is easy—you merely reveal chronologically how the particular advocate started on such and such a ground and, when challenged by facts, had to shift to another position.

Argument from Tradition and Custom

Many people tend to be instinctively cautious and conservative. They tend to do things in a traditional fashion; customs control their behavior. Thus, the advocate who argues that we have always done things that way and that it is the traditional and customary way will have strong influence. The assumption is that if we have done things that way for a long time, it must have been a good way. This appeal, without additional argument and evidence to support it, however, is fallacious. To do things always in the traditional fashion or the customary fashion would bring no progress, no change. Furthermore, good reasons supported by evidence should be given to continue to do things in exactly the same fashion as has been done in the past. For years America avoided entangling foreign alliances because Thomas Jefferson said we should. The basis of the argument on tradition and custom is that because our ancestors did it that way, we should do it that way. The fallacy lies in the fact that conditions change and what was true for one generation is not necessarily true for later ones.

Exposing this fallacy can be rather difficult because it has considerable power. Probably the best way to overcome such conservatism is to suggest that if humankind had been unwilling to give up the old sailing ships for Robert Fulton's steamboat, we would never have had the great ocean liners of today; that the automobile would never have replaced the horse and buggy; that the airplane would never have been developed so that we can travel across the ocean in a few hours. In picking your examples, choose ones that are very obvious and choose those more closely related to the field of discussion.

An Appeal to the Ignorance of the Opposite

"This is true because you can't prove the opposite; there is no evidence to the contrary." When this claim is made, the advocate commits the fallacy of an appeal to ignorance of the opposite, which is based on false assumptions. It assumes that in every gathering someone will be present who knows all the facts of the subject that is being discussed both pro and con. Obviously this cannot be true. We are all far too ignorant of too many subjects for this to occur. Nevertheless, this is the first assumption of the person who commits this fallacy. The second assumption is that studies have been made of all things in the universe and that humankind has all the evidence available. This, too, is a false assumption; many things have not yet been studied thoroughly or studied at all. Even in many cases where studies have been made, not all aspects of the problem have been examined or uncovered.

Fortunately, this particular appeal is less effective the more educated your audience is. It is, however, a difficult fallacy to expose. One tactic is to reveal the false assumptions on which the claim is based. Another method is similar to the one described above in exposing the falseness of the argument from tradition and custom. This method is to cite examples where the application of that principle appears ridiculous. In your refutation you can appeal to the audience in this fashion: "Because there is no evidence to show that I didn't commit a crime is no proof that I did commit one." Or, "In the days before Christopher Columbus, people believed the world was flat. Just because there was no proof the world was round didn't make the world flat." In choosing examples, make sure that they be obviously ridiculous in their application of the principle and get them as closely related to the subject as possible.

False Synthesis

This is the fallacy of assuming that what is true of the parts is true of the whole. It is readily illustrated in the field of athletics where all star basketball or baseball teams are not necessarily great simply because each of the athletes on the team is great. They may readily lack such traits as teamwork and an understanding of how to adapt to each other. Certainly teams without individual stars may become great teams simply through their highly developed teamwork and ability to complement one another, as well as having developed strong team spirit. Another example: although examples of provincialism and narrowness are found in all parts of the country, the conclusion isn't necessarily that the country as a whole is provincial and narrow.

You can expose this particular fallacy in several ways. One method is to utilize the facts that will demonstrate that the conclusion is not true. A second is by reasoning from analogy, offering examples in areas other than the subject at hand where weakness in the parts did not mean that the whole was weak or vice versa. Still another way is to reveal the false assumptions on which the argument is based.

Fallacy of Division

This fallacy is the converse of the fallacy of false synthesis—what was true of the whole is also true of the parts. In many a progressive nation some of the parts may be quite backward. Certainly we could call the European Union progressive, yet it contains several backward areas. Because a rope is strong does not mean that each separate strand has unusual strength. Because a certain school is a great university does not mean that each of the students attending or even graduating is a great scholar. The methods of exposing this fallacy are the same as for false synthesis, i.e., utilizing facts to the contrary, reasoning from analogy, or revealing the false assumptions.

Fallacy of Equivocation

Many words have two or more meanings. The fallacy of equivocation occurs when a word with two or more meanings is used in the development of a particular argument. We have already defined *equivocation* under deduction in discussing the fallacy of four terms, and several examples were given. The fallacy of equivocation occurs particularly in arguments involving words that have a multiplicity of meanings, such as *capitalism, government regulation, inflation, depression, expansion,* and *progress.* This fallacy may sometimes be committed when the debater is cornered and is trying to find a way out. A person caught in the act of gossiping may equivocate by suggesting that he was sharing information with his friends.

To expose the fallacy of equivocation, you give accurate and specific definitions of terms, and show carefully that in one place the definition of the terms was different from the definition in another. A word of caution: you must be very certain that you have listened carefully to the argument of your opponent to make sure that she actually used a word in two different senses.

REFUTATION BY SPECIAL METHODS

This chapter would not be complete without a discussion of certain special methods of refutation that can be very effective devices to put across your point of view.

Reducing the Argument to an Absurdity (*Reductio ad Absurdum*)

This weapon is extremely powerful in the hands of a skillful user. Once learned, the process is rather simple: the general principle on which the argument of the individual is based is presented and then, by applying it to specific cases, made to appear ridiculous. Benjamin Franklin used this very effectively in refuting the argument that a person should own property to be able to vote. He first stated the principle and then applied it thus: "You say I should own property in order to vote; supposing I own a jackass, I then own property and thus I can vote. But suppose I sell the jackass; I no longer own property, and therefore I cannot vote. Thus, the vote represents not me but the jackass." Earlier in this chapter, without naming the method, we advised that reducing an argument to an absurdity was a powerful means for exposing the fallacy of argument from tradition and custom and the fallacy of an appeal to the ignorance of the opposite. In demonstrating the effectiveness of this tool, some of our great principles of conduct can be made to seem ridiculous. For example, telling the truth is recognized as a principle of conduct worth observing. However, telling our hostess that we hate her and had a miserable time at her party is to reduce the principle to absurdity. Here a debater refutes the principle by putting it in a situation that is ridiculous. Practice finding and wording the general principle behind the argument and then applying it to specific occasions where it is ridiculous.

Adopting Opposing Arguments (Turning the Tables)

One of the most powerful tools by which you can influence an audience is to use the evidence, the premises, or other statements of opponents to support your own case. You can employ this technique in both refutation and in counter-refutation. Damaging admissions or statements usually appear in issues other than the one being discussed at the moment. Often an advocate, in trying to demonstrate that no serious objections to her new proposal will be voiced, will make statements that are grave admissions that the solution itself might not be as effective as alleged. Or, in discussion of a later issue, she may make statements that will be virtual admissions that the evils are not great enough to demand a change. If you are alert all the way through the discourse of another person, you will often find such statements, which may become powerful support for your own arguments.

As we have said, the chances to use the technique of turning the tables or adopting opposing arguments are many. In debating the proposition, "We should close down nuclear generators because of potential for accidents," opponents often use evidence that the danger is not significant enough to worry about. This evidence in itself contains the implication that, if the danger were greater, it would be a grave concern. When those opposed go even further and suggest means of preventing nuclear accidents, those favoring the ban can use that as additional evidence that the danger is so great that something ought to be done about it. The speaker who is alert to all of the ramifications of the statements of another will find frequent chances to make use of the evidence, arguments, or statements he supplies to support his case. A word of warning: Be sure to quote your opponents accurately and within the context of their statements. The implication that even they didn't realize how much they admitted has a strong influence on audiences.

Method of Residues

This special method of refutation was discussed in part in the chapter on analysis. Let us note further that the process is one of setting up a disjunction in which several, not just two, choices are suggested. All these choices should be carefully enumerated and all should also be mutually exclusive in order to avoid the two fallacies of disjunction.

This special method should be used only in those cases in which members of the audience may have strong preferences for some of the solutions or courses of action that you would like to discourage. It is a subtle way of refuting opposing points of view without being too obvious and has the further advantage of following the technique of discussion in which various solutions are usually explored in order to find the best one.

An example of the use of method of residues occurred in a small town in Vermont. Increased school population forced the citizens of the town to try to solve the problem of housing all the children, since the small building held both the high school and the grade school. Utilizing the method of residues, the speaker advocated the least popular of all solutions. Among courses of action enumerated was a suggestion to enlarge the present building, which had the disadvantage of resulting in a very poorly planned building and a great lack of playground space. A second alternative was to form a union school with nearby towns. This was the popular solution but, as the speaker suggested, the nearby towns had voted down this solution. A third solution was to build a new high school in a new location. This alternative was pointed out to be a very poor one because it would be very costly for only 80 students and because so small a high school would fail to provide maximum opportunities for education. Finally, the speaker came down to her unpopular solution, which was to send the high school students into the closest city as tuition students until such time as a union school could be formed with some other town. In this case, the method of residues was used to remind members of the audience of the strong disadvantages of the other solutions that some of them favored. In this case, the choice of the use of the method of residues was wise. On the other hand, you will waste time if you use this method if there is no need for it. In many cases calling to the attention of members of the audience other solutions is unwise because it may only reinforce disfavor of your advocacy.

To counter this technique, you should try to note if other possible alternatives are available. Furthermore, you might try to see if the alternatives are mutually exclusive; in other words, could all of them or a combination of them be used? A speaker discussing solutions to the problem of financing schools suggested three courses of action: consolidation, increased state aid, and federal aid. He ended up by advocating the third. The speaker countering him utilized both of these suggested methods of refutation. First, she suggested another alternative, that increasing local support for education was possible. Then she went on to point out that the various alternatives need not be mutually exclusive, that increased local, state, and federal aid to education combined might be the best solution of all. Thus she successfully countered her opponent's attempt to use the method of residues.

The Dilemma

Pointing out a dilemma is another strong weapon for refutation. To use this technique, you must show that the arguments of the advocate can lead to only two results, two solutions, or two courses of action, both of which are untenable. Each of these alternatives is usually called a "horn." Here again, disjunction is involved. The dilemma is a strong one if the alternatives are both bad. The following is a traditional story illustrating the dilemma.

> A young woman made a contract with a teacher to learn law. The stipulations were that the young woman, who was without funds, would pay for her lessons after winning her first case in court. Unfortunately for the teacher, after the lessons were through and the young woman had learned the law completely, she decided not to practice. So the teacher sued for payment. He expected to catch the student in the following dilemma: "If the court decides in my favor, the young woman will have to pay because the court has decided that she must pay. Therefore, I will get my money. On the other hand, if the court decides against me, then the young woman will have won her first case in court and by the terms of the contract will have to pay. Thus I will get my money." This was the case put before the court. The young woman, however, was a true student of the teacher. She built her refutation around this dilemma: "Should the court decide in my favor that I don't have to pay, I won't have to pay, and therefore I won't. On the other hand, if the court decides in favor of my teacher, the terms of the contract will hold, for I still will not have won my first case in court and thus, according to contract, I won't have to pay."

How the court decided is unknown. One can readily see the difficulty of deciding the case.

Dilemmas occur more often than we may think. When a situation arises wherein the result will be untenable whatever course of action is pursued, we are said to be "impaled on the horns of a dilemma." Alternatives are not always limited to two; the number of undesirable alternatives may be three, in which case we find ourselves in a "trilemma"; with four unpleasant alternatives, we might be impaled on the horns of a "tetralemma." More than four and you are involved in a "polylemma." The small Vermont town mentioned above found itself in a situation of a polylemma. It couldn't continue with the present school because space was inadequate; it couldn't consolidate because the other towns wouldn't agree; it didn't want to put up a new building because of the expense and the resulting school would be too small to offer greatest educational opportunities. Sending the students to the neighboring city involved issues of transportation costs, less likelihood of participation in extracurricular activities because of the distance, and because many of its students might feel lost in such a large high school.

Various ways are available to you in your attempt to counter a dilemma. One method is to suggest a new alternative that avoids the undesirable features of the proposed alternatives. Thus, the first fallacy to look for in countering the dilemma is the fallacy of failing to mention all the possible choices. A second method would be to challenge the proof of the disadvantages of one or the other of the two alternatives. If the person who develops the dilemma fails to prove the strong disadvantages of each of the horns, the dilemma has little strength. On the other hand, if you are able to minimize the undesirable factors of one of the alternatives and point out its strong advantages, the effect of the conundrum of the dilemma on the audience will be lessened or even destroyed. A third way would be to introduce a new set of arguments that avoid the supposed dilemma. For example, in the dilemma of the young woman and her teacher of law, the case might be decided on the basis of the moral obligation of any individual under any circumstances to pay for services agreed to and rendered.

Exposing Inconsistencies

Whenever a speaker in developing a speech makes a statement in one part that contradicts or is opposite to a statement in another part of the speech, he is guilty of being inconsistent. In exposing such inconsistencies by pointing out that the speaker promises one thing to one group and the contrary to another group, you weaken his arguments. Falling into inconsistencies or apparent inconsistencies is easy. The campaign speaker making certain promises to consumers may readily become inconsistent when she advocates a course of action that does not take these promises into account when addressing a group of merchants. Frequently a law that aids consumers takes away some privileges from merchants. Promising consumers lower prices and then promising merchants greater profits is an inconsistency.

Knowledge of where these inconsistencies are apt to occur will help. Many speakers tend to emphasize the great need for a change and then minimize the objectionable results that can be expected from their solution. A speaker who is prone to exaggerate at any point in her speaking may fall into an inconsistency when she is attacked. An advocate who suggests an evil in the present system and then proposes a solution that has little causal force in removing that evil is apt to fall into inconsistency. For example, a speaker who gives broken homes as the main cause of juvenile crime, and then offers as a solution the development of new recreation centers is at least guilty of being muddy in her thinking if not inconsistent. Those opposing any change in the present policy often find themselves falling into inconsistencies. First they will claim that there is no need to change. If forced to suggest a plan of repairs or a substitute plan, they will be definitely inconsistent. Or again, a speaker who is opposed to a change and claims first of all that there is no need for a change and then attacks the proposed solution of the advocate on the ground that it will not remove evils (having stated there are none) may find himself quite inconsistent in his use of language. Being aware of where people are likely to fall into inconsistencies in using argument will help you discover them quickly and help you develop your skill in exposing them effectively.

To avoid inconsistencies is a matter of care and accuracy in analyzing your problem and checking to see that you are consistent throughout. Certainly as a defense lawyer you would have to decide whether you are going to try to defend your client by a not guilty plea or by the plea that she is not guilty by reason of insanity. You can hardly do both. In the same fashion, you can hardly offer a plan of repairs and at the same time suggest that there is absolutely no need to change at all. Careful choice of language and careful wording of the exact stand that you intend to take on a proposition can avoid apparent inconsistencies. The clever person can, in countering a new proposal, use what is called an "even if" case. Here the debater is very careful to point out that such and such is his stand but should there be those in the audience who have been convinced by some of the arguments, at least he would urge them not to go any further than a modest plan of repairs. One can avoid the inconsistency of the statement, "The plan of the advocate will not remove the evils," by saying that the proposed solution will bring no significant improvement over the present system.

Use caution in choosing to expose the inconsistencies of others. Many times the alleged inconsistency just doesn't exist. Either the person exposing the alleged inconsistency took a sentence completely out of its context or she failed to listen carefully in the first place. If you fall into these errors, you will harm yourself far more than the person you are attacking. Be sure that the inconsistency is real, that you have listened carefully to what was said, and that you are not taking phrases or sentences out of context.

Exposing Irrelevant Arguments

An irrelevant argument has little or nothing to do with the proposition or issue under discussion. A discussion of whether a certain individual has been a good person all her life has little relevancy to whether she committed this particular murder. At least one can suggest that it is irrelevant. The argument that corporations are outsourcing jobs has little relevancy to the issue of whether legislation is needed to curb auto emissions. Irrelevant arguments arise from many causes. One is poor definition, another is weakness in analysis. A third is a deliberate attempt on the part of the speaker to divert attention from weaknesses to strengths. Often irrelevant arguments arise when a speaker tries to cover up a weakness by appealing to prejudice. Still a fourth cause of introduction of irrelevant materials is the inability of some speakers to refute. As they are unprepared or unable to counter arguments directly, they will try to divert attention by going off on a tangent.

To expose the irrelevant argument, you show the failure of the individual to speak on the subject as you defined it or show that he is unwilling to meet the issue as you have accurately worded it. Or you can expose it by showing that she was unable to answer your argument directly and thus turned to appeals to prejudice. Still another way of exposing irrelevant arguments is to show that they refer to common ground that is conceded by all and is not a part of the discussion at the moment. Following is an example of a combination of the first and last methods.

Our arguments were presented to show that the method of representation by population was fairer than representation by jurisdiction. The gentleperson in challenging our arguments went into a long discourse of statistics showing how perfect equality and fairness cannot be achieved. All this is true. But the issue before us is not whether perfection can be achieved. The issue is which of the methods is fairer under the conditions we are facing. On this issue the speaker did not choose to say anything.

Exercises

1. Define:

   a. Refutation

   b. Counter-refutation

   c. Fallacy

2. Explain each of the following methods of refutation:

   a. Refutation by challenging analysis

   b. Refutation by challenging definition

   c. Refutation through minimizing

   d. Counter-refutation by maximizing

   e. Refutation by denying the evidence

   f. Refutation by exposing fallacies in reasoning

   g. Refutation by demonstrating the opposite

3. Bring to class written examples of each of the above methods of refutation, using newspaper editorials, essays, or written copies of speeches as the material to refute.

4. Demonstrate each of the above methods by refuting speeches of classmates.

5. Listen to an intercollegiate debate noting whenever any of the above methods are used. Be ready to report them to the class.

6. Explain each of the following special types of fallacies:

   a. Arguing in a circle

   b. Assuming a more general truth that involves the point at issue

   c. The fallacious question

   d. Appeals to prejudice

e. Argument involving personalities (argumentum ad hominem)

f. Shifting ground

g. Argument from tradition and custom

h. An appeal to ignorance of the opposite

i. False synthesis

j. Fallacy of division

k. Fallacy of equivocation

7. Give an example of each of the above fallacies.

8. Explain how each of the special fallacies may be exposed. Use the examples in Exercise 7 to illustrate your explanation.

9. Explain each of the following special methods of refutation:

a. *Reductio ad absurdum*

b. Adopting opposing arguments (turning the tables)

c. Method of residues

d. The dilemma

e. Exposing inconsistencies

f. Exposing irrelevant arguments

10. Reduce each of the following wise sayings into an absurdity:

a. It is better to have tried and failed than never to have tried at all.

b. Honesty is the best policy.

11. Give examples of how you might "turn the tables" on arguments presented by your classmates.

12. Give a speech favoring some solution toward which your audience is hostile; use "method of residues" to make it more acceptable.

13. One of the best ways to counter a new proposal is to build "dilemma" objections such as, "In order to build a program strong enough to remove the evils it will cost so much that we can't afford it." Build one or more dilemma objections to some new proposal and present them to the class.

14. Utilize one or more methods of countering a dilemma in refuting the preceding speeches.

15. Answer the following about "exposing inconsistencies":

a. Why is there a great likelihood that an advocate will become inconsistent in her development of the "need" and "will remove the need" issues, if she isn't careful?

b. Why must an opponent of a new proposal be careful to avoid inconsistencies in his development of the same two issues?

c. Why may an opponent of a new proposal fall into inconsistencies if she minimizes the need and then suggests there are great objections to the proposal?

d. Why may an opponent of a new proposal fall into inconsistencies if he claims small benefits from a new proposal, yet also claim it will bring great objections?

e. Why may an advocate of a new proposal fall into inconsistencies by claiming great new benefits and then claim it will be easy to put the new proposal into operation?

16. Give a prepared speech of advocacy to the class, have a classmate evaluate or refute it, then counter his evaluation or refutation by revealing to the audience any irrelevancies that he may have fallen into.

Chapter 11
Logic Is Not Enough: Use Other Sources of Persuasion, Too

Throughout this volume we have been explaining the various ways to use logic in influencing others, which is argumentation. Logic is only one of the constituent elements of persuasion and you cannot depend on it alone. We have to convince people to believe that which logic suggests they ought to believe. Those who depend on logic alone will be disappointed in their results.

CONSTITUENT ELEMENTS IN PERSUASION: LOGOS, PATHOS, ETHOS, AND STYLE

This particular classification of the constituent elements of persuasion was derived from the Greeks. Aristotle used them as the basis for his volume on rhetoric. Logos, often called the "logical element of persuasion," is that element of persuasion in which logic is used to influence others. Pathos is that element of persuasion in which psychological or emotional factors are used to influence others. It could be called "the psychological mode of persuasion," or the "pathetic proofs." Ethos is that element of persuasion arising from the influence of the speaker; the factors of speech delivery, personality, and position or reputation in life. Style is that element of persuasion derived from the power of language to influence others. Choice of words that make a speech vivid, sentence structure, and other rhetorical devices constitute style. The full power of a particular speech is derived from the successful combination of these four elements and is modified by the attitudes and conditions of the members of your audience. In fact, we could almost suggest the following formula: Logos plus pathos plus ethos plus stylistic devices modified by the conditioning and attitudes of the audience equal the results you get.

This Chapter—A Suggested Outline for Further Study

In this volume we have endeavored to uncover the elements and basic principles involved in influencing others through argument, but a single volume cannot possibly cover all these other elements adequately. Each of the other elements is equally important, so in this chapter, therefore, we will merely give a suggested outline of these.

Pathos: Psychological or Emotional Appeals

As persuasion is the art of influencing others and because psychological or emotional appeals are so important, we must first understand the steps in persuasion. W.N. Brigance suggests these three steps: "Capture the attention of the audience, arouse the wants, produce the response."[1] A.H. Monroe breaks them down into five steps: "Capture the attention of the audience, show the need, satisfy that need, visualize the future if accepted, and direct the action."[2] Briefly, these are broken down into the attention step, the need step, the satisfaction step, the visualization step, and the action step. These must be studied because they are the basis of the psychological appeals that you will use in speech.

Capturing and Holding Attention

All writers in the field agree that capturing and holding the attention of the audience are essential to successful speaking. Much has been written in the area of attention both by psychologists and by writers in the field of speech. In addressing an audience you should keep in mind certain facts about getting attention and holding it. You will have captured the attention of the audience when you have all of them concentrated on you and what you are saying. The audience gives involuntary attention to you when you walk on the stage or

---

1. *Speech Composition*, 2nd ed. (New York: Appleton Century Crofts, 1953), 101.

2. *Principles and Styles of Speeches*, 4th ed. (New York: Scott, Foresman, 1955), 62.

someone starts a meeting. Such involuntary attention to some object we call "primary attention." At other times, we may have to force ourselves to pay attention. We are then giving "secondary attention." A third form—"derived primary attention"—occurs when what once caused us to give secondary attention becomes so interesting that we involuntarily listen: The person who had to force himself to pay attention in chemistry class and paid attention so long that he became interested enough to become a chemical engineer has reached the stage where he involuntarily pays attention to things chemical in nature. This is an example of derived primary attention and illustrates the very important principle: Interest grows with knowledge. As a speaker, you will use certain elements that will bring you involuntary, or primary, attention and then you will do everything in your power to give enough facts and picture your ideas so vividly for your audience that you can hold their attention. The use of the stylistic elements is as important in holding the attention of an audience as emotional factors.

Every good speaker needs to develop knowledge of those factors that hold attention and to develop skill in the use of them. To what do we pay attention? We are interested in the satisfaction of our basic wants and desires and in what is familiar. In fact, if what the speaker is discussing is too foreign and strange to us, we will soon lose interest. The novel or new has the power to excite. People capture our attention: who they are, what they are doing, their problems, their enjoyments. Notice how often businesses put people into the advertisement for the goods they are trying to sell. Conflict has power to capture and hold attention particularly when the conflict is strong—consider the millions of spectators at sporting events. Things that antagonize us hold our attention to such a degree that some speakers have even used this device for a brief period at the beginning of a speech as a means of capturing the attention and getting the audience interested in following them all the way through. In using such a technique, the speaker will briefly do that which will antagonize and then turn around and attack that which first antagonized. New adventures intrigue us and capture our fancy.

On the other hand, within the speech proper the speaker can make use of other factors of attention. Humor will not only attract our attention when used early in the speech but will have power to hold attention or recapture it from time to time throughout. Avoid creating an appetite for it, however. Deliberately injecting suspense into the speech, so that your audience will wonder how things are going to come out, holds attention. The speaker should be quite aware of the use of climax because attention is held more strongly when the speech is rising from one climax to a second and on to a final climax. Movement or action both in delivering the speech and within the thought content of the speech will help hold attention. The use of action verbs (forecasts, summaries) will keep the speech moving toward a goal and that very movement will tend to help hold the attention of the audience to the end. The subject matter of the speech should be vital to the listeners; without this, the audience will lose interest. The solving of problems or riddles captures the attention of many. The speaker can call attention to an effect searching for a cause or call attention to a cause searching for an effect. Or you can play up the problem raising the question continuously, "What is the solution? Where do we go from here?"

In addition, elements of the dramatic will help you bring your ideas to life. Specific time, specific place, characters, dialogue, and conflict, the overcoming of obstacles, suspense, and climax can all be used to great effect. Whenever your speech can become a story of an idea it will help. Furthermore, human beings are interested in what appeals to the senses, what we can see, hear, feel, touch, smell. Thus, the use of visual aids in the form of PowerPoint and other computer presentations, models, or actual objects helps capture and sustain attention.

Appeals to Basic Wants

Humankind's greatest concern is to live. We need food, clothing, shelter, love of friends and family, success, money, sexual satisfaction, a home, and to avoid death. The list is extensive, and the most basic wants are essential to life and to health. Most of our time is spent in satisfying these basic wants. Our strongest consideration in choosing our vocation or profession is which one will best satisfy these wants. The great speaker is one who understands these basic wants and can then adapt them in her speeches from audience to audience. A salesperson will hardly get rich selling skis to the aged. Thus, the first type and the strongest of all emotional appeals are appeals to the basic wants, particularly the ones of the audience you are addressing at the moment.

Appeals to Blocked Wants—The Hate Object

From time to time catastrophes in the form of economic depressions, wars, and defeat in wars befall nations. When these occur, the basic wants of many within the nation remain unsatisfied. For example, in a depression great numbers of people may be looking for work and cannot find it, and thus are blocked in the satisfaction of their basic desires for food, clothing, and shelter.

Under such circumstances, the public speaker in charging "they are denying us the chance to get food, clothing and shelter, to get work" is addressing an audience ready to listen. A reservoir of emotion easily turned into hate or fear can quickly be tapped. This "blocked wants" appeal is probably the strongest of all that can be made.

In addition to this appeal and often reinforcing the blocked wants appeal is the focusing of the attention of the audience on some hate object, which is pointed out to be the cause of many of their difficulties. The strong communist threat after World War II caused many fears to arise within the people of the Western world. Huge increases in taxes necessary to support and build a large military machine denied many the necessities and luxuries of life. The Soviet Union and its leaders easily became the hate object for the people of the Western world, particularly those in the United States. The realistic presence of the communist threat and the consequent increase in taxes made it easy for the speaker to tap this emotional reservoir of hate. Hitler used another notable example of this hate object appeal in his rise to power in Germany. The terrific depression after Germany's defeat in World War I, followed by the breakdown in currency and consequent unemployment blocked the wants for food, clothing, and shelter for many Germans. The hate objects of the Versailles Treaty and the Jews made Hitler's appeals unusually strong. Many people blocked in their personal desires and problems are continually arising within nations, thus the world has many whose wants are being blocked. The blocked wants appeal along with the hate object is usually available to some degree in every society, and the effective public speaker should be aware of this and be alert to its possible ethical use.

Appeals to Symbols of Identification

Freedom of speech, freedom of the press, the right to worship as we please are ideals for each of us who live in a democracy. Through teaching and experience, these symbols of identification become as important to us as food, clothing, and shelter. The War in Iraq to "spread democracy to the Middle East" is an example. Those ideas and concepts become as important to us as the satisfaction of basic wants. In the political world, we are concerned with freedom of speech, press, and religion. In our economic life, we respond to the phrase, "private ownership." In our religious life, we believe in following the Golden Rule.

Symbols of identification differ from basic wants in that they are a part of our cultural heritage, they are not inborn. In our homes, schools, churches, and other institutions we are taught these until they become a part of us, and a threat to them is often as strong a threat as to our lives. We have fought wars to retain them or defend them. In many cases, these symbols of identification become the basis on which our arguments are built.

Appeals to Emotionally Loaded Words

Many words become rich in emotional connotation for us because of what we have been taught and because of our experience. Some words, when merely voiced or printed, engender strong positive emotional reactions, while others bring feelings of negation or revulsion. For most people, such words as *home, father, mother, church, patriotism* bring a warm, positive emotional reactions. Other words, such as *traitor, hell, enemy, cheat,* bring negative emotional reactions. These words are designated variously—some call them "stereotypes" and include within them the symbols of identification discussed in the paragraph above. Others have called them "positive sanctions" and "negative sanctions." Positive sanctions are those that bring warm or strong positive emotional reactions, while negative sanctions are those that bring revulsion. In this connection we should note the stronger emotional reaction that some words will bring compared with others that have a similar meaning. The word *home* brings a much stronger emotional reaction than the word *house.* The words *father* or *mother* are stronger emotionally than the word parent. We should note further that in some cases individuals would not have the same emotional reactions. An individual who has had a miserable home and a horrible set of experiences with her mother will not react positively to those words. We should be aware of these exceptions, although in the main we may use them in a positive sense. You may find it profitable to base your argument on various emotionally loaded words. Used properly throughout the speech, they can season it with an emotional color that will enrich it.

Appeals to Sentiments

Attributes that describe the desirable type of behavior in humankind cause us to react favorably toward people and sometimes toward things. These attributes include such characteristics as honesty, sincerity, conscientiousness, reliability, industriousness, justice, courage, friendliness, dependability, and so on. The appeal of the "good old times" is also available to you. You may find it profitable to base your arguments on these appeals to sentiments, such as the sense of fair play, justice, and honesty. These somewhat idealized concepts will often reinforce your argument. This is particularly true when you are concerned with the praise or the blame of a specific individual. The opposite of each of these sentiments or the lack of it brings a negative emotional response. Like emotionally loaded words, these sentiments can be used as a seasoning throughout the speech.

Associated-Attitude Appeal

Whenever your audience analysis indicates that many of your hearers are hostile to your proposition, you should consider building a speech utilizing the associated-attitude appeal. An attitude can be defined as a predisposition to act and is the result of all the teaching and experiences we have had about and with a particular concept. Our beliefs are the verbalization of those attitudes, while our opinions can be defined as the oral or written expression of our beliefs. An associated attitude is one that is relevant to, yet not a basic part of, the structure of a particular attitude. The process of using this appeal is to focus the attention of the audience on a particular attitude toward which they are distinctly favorable. Once you have centered the positive reactions on this attitude, you can then associate it with the attitude toward which they would be hostile. An excellent example of this kind of appeal is the "Liverpool Address" by Henry Ward Beecher. During the American Civil War, Beecher went to Europe to get a favorable reaction of the British toward the cause of the North. The blockade by the North of the South's ports had stopped the flow of cotton from the South to the British cotton mills, so that many of them had been closed. To his audience at Liverpool, Beecher was an object associated with their unemployment. Knowing the audience would be antagonistic, Beecher used the associated-attitude approach. He called attention to the strong British attitudes concerning fair play and giving a person a fair hearing. Thus he began, but he utilized this associated-attitude appeal all the way through—his whole speech was built on the concept that they needed a market for their goods and the North could provide that market. He associated the desire on the part of all to have good markets for their products with the people of the North. Thus he was able to get a fair hearing. Should you find yourself in a situation where your audience is quite hostile, make use of the associated-attitude appeal in your argument.

Appeals to Prejudice

Appeals to prejudice are those based on the hatreds and likes that people have formed with insufficient grounds. Prejudice, as we have noted, comes from the words pre and judge, or "to judge with insufficient facts." They are lean-ings toward or against something with insufficient evidence. Often speakers make use of appeals to prejudice. The dislike or even hatred between the white and black, the Jew and gentile, the Catholic and Protestant, management and labor, the rich and the poor is utilized to arouse the audience emotionally. Your authors do not recommend your use of this type of appeal. Unfortunately, in unguarded moments, many have used it. Some speakers have felt that a worthy end justifies using this appeal as the means of attaining it, and some-times campaign speakers under the stress of a close and hard fought campaign may fall into its use. Inasmuch as we have formed conclusions on so many sub-jects without having sufficient grounds, prejudice is difficult to avoid. Accord-ingly, appeals to prejudice are difficult to avoid. At least you should know what appeals to prejudice are, be able to identify them for audiences, and be able to expose them as they are chiefly the result of the fallacy of hasty generalization and lack of knowledge.

Other Factors in Pathos

The foregoing appeals are the most common and most frequently used. There are additional ones. You should know, for instance, that rationalization forms the basis of most selling, that a salesperson of an article or an idea frequently is merely providing the reasons that a customer may use to satisfy a spouse, a parent, or a banker for buying a particular thing. You should know that distin-guishing between rationalization and reasoning can be very difficult because many good speeches, particularly sales speeches, have as their purpose the provision of a set of reasons (rationalizations) for the buyer. Other appeals take the form of "getting on the bandwagon," or use "glittering generalities," "the plain folks" approach, and "we are in this together" appeal. The good speaker also needs to know what elements are involved in suggestion and how to render an audience suggestible, as well as the various elements essential to developing the psychological unity of the audience.

How to Use Emotional Appeals with Argumentative Speeches

Emotional appeals for capturing and holding attention must be understood and used throughout the speech. Each of the other types of appeals is used in a similar fashion in the main headings, within the support material, in the conclusion, and in the introduction. These other types of appeals are used in the following specific ways:

Appeals in Main Headings. Whatever appeals you are using should be worded in the sentence that represents the main heading. The following headings certainly have no basic emotional appeal:

> There is a need for a change.
>
> Our plan will solve the need.
>
> Our plan is practical.

This threefold wording of the main headings will certainly not appeal to anyone's emotions.

Consider the appeal of Henry Ward Beecher's main headings. They were:

> You need a market for your goods.
>
> The North can provide that market.
>
> The South cannot.

Or again, consider the speaker who is trying to convince her audience to refrain from buying on credit. The following are obviously poor:

> Credit buying is uneconomical.
>
> Credit buying is bad for a rising economy.
>
> Credit buying is bad for a falling economy.

The following are certainly much better:

> Credit buying costs too much.
>
> Credit buying makes inflation worse.
>
> Credit buying makes depression worse.

The appeals to cost, bad inflation, and bad depressions tend to arouse the audience emotionally. Certainly they are much stronger emotionally than the first set. Headings like the following, once proved, can arouse emotionally as well as stimulate intellectually:

> This law threatens freedom of the press.
>
> They threaten to destroy our homes.
>
> She is a woman of courage.

Your main headings must be worded to include one of these appeals within it. Other things being equal, the stronger the appeal, the more stimulating the argument.

Use in the Development of Each Argument. Because each argument must be based on some emotional appeal, the development of each will be geared to that appeal. Call attention to the basic appeal as you explain the point; as you develop it by using additional support material, you may repeat an appeal often. Sometimes you will refer to it each time you add a new piece of support material. Or the repetition may be mere seasoning so that the point of the argument will not be lost. Sometimes in the development of an argument the "what harm" or "so what" part is left until last. With this structure, the development of the emotional base of the argument is left to the spot where the what harm argument is developed. In fact, the very definition of what is "harmful" occurs when you can explain that people are "denied food, clothing, and shelter" because of the policy you are deploring. The climax of the development of an argument often depends on the use of additional support material to show the pervasiveness of the harm. In other words, the climax of a particular argument will show how quantitatively strong the harm is. Remember that the climax is a function of the emotional appeal, hardly ever of pure intellectual stimulation.

Emotional Appeals in the Conclusion. The conclusion will frequently contain a summary of the main headings, thus you will have a repetition of the appeals as worded in the main headings. The conclusion is actually a virtual climax of the speech, a bringing back of all the power of the speech at once into the minds of the audience, and should be rich in emotional overtones all the way through. A great weakness of many speakers is that they ramble through the conclusion rather than realizing that this is the point at which the audience should feel overpowered by the specific purpose of the speaker. The closing part of the conclusion should be a strong, personal, emotional appeal to each listener. Here, particularly, make use of a restrained appeal to the sentiments. A word of caution: Overuse can destroy the effect; restraint can be powerful; understatement can strengthen; exaggeration can destroy.

Psychological Factors Within the Introduction. The very psychology of the introduction of any speech is to capture the attention of the audience for a subject, to make them want to listen to a discussion of it, and to develop the prestige of the speaker. Strong appeals are out of the question in the introduction because no development of the subject has yet occurred. Added to this will be the problem of arousing the interest of the audience to listen to a discussion of the topic. At this point you may allude to those emotional appeals that you intend to develop in the discussion. This is a restrained type of development and more of a focusing of attention on these basic attitudes or wants than a definite appeal. For example, a speaker discussing buying on credit may raise questions hoping to arouse the audience's interest in hearing the discussion. These questions might well be: "How costly is credit buying? Does it cost us too much? Does it have any serious effects on depressions? Does it have any influence on inflation?" Such questions may give rise to the desire on the part of the audience to hear you discuss that topic.

Some speakers, on the other hand, will develop the emotional basis for an argument or for the whole speech in the introduction. For example, a speaker opposed to an affirmative action law spent some time in her introduction laying her emotional base in stating that only those laws are fair or just which punish all of the guilty equally. By comparison and example she laid down this basic premise that was the overall emotional appeal for her later arguments. The discussion then consisted of condemning the law on the grounds that often the employees and customers of an employer drive the employer to discriminate on the basis of race, creed, or color. In addition, the argument was advanced that the law was unfair on the grounds that it punished the employer only and could do nothing to the customers or the employees. Important to note here is the principle used in building a speech, namely, that in the introduction the speaker may uncover the emotional base for the whole speech that is to follow.

A restrained use of emotionally loaded words is often effective in the introduction. At other times you may wish to make use of the "plain folks appeal" and "the bandwagon appeal"—suggesting that everybody is thinking and talking about the topic.

In general, then, in the introduction you will make strong use of those factors that will focus the attention of the audience on your subject; you will arouse the desire of the audience to hear the subject being discussed; you may set up the emotional base for the whole speech; you will utilize a restrained sprinkling of emotionally loaded words; and you may use other types of modest appeals, such as "everybody is discussing it" and "the plain folks approach."

Style: Making the Speech Pictorial, Vivid, Stirring

The study of making your speech vivid will repay you throughout your career by making you a more effective, more compelling advocate. Something is vivid when it has the power to excite the senses. The word *skunk* brings quickly to mind the image of the little black-and-white furry animal that can expel an unusually strong odor. The odor is so strong that it excites the senses. Beautiful colors excite the eyes. Beautiful music will excite through the ears, while the images of good food will appeal to the taste. The purpose of the study of style is to discover how to make the speech vivid, how to make it summon up mental pictures, how to excite the audience to response. The following are some of the major factors involved.

Choosing Effective Words

The most effective words for the speaker are not those multisyllable, infrequently used words; rather they are the frequently used simple words. Your audience must immediately understand your meaning—these words will do the job.

Image-Bearing Words. Consider using image-bearing words, words that immediately stir up images in the minds of the hearers. Specific words like *skunk, hitchhiker,* and *Atilla the Hun* stir up clearer images than the more general words *animal, traveler,* and *famous nomad.* In a speech, say, "You will become a Washington, a Lincoln, a Jefferson," rather than, "You will become a great person." Your speech will be more vivid if you deliberately seek and use those words that stir up specific and accurate images. Remember, as a speaker, you are trying to paint pictures with words. The abstract will seldom stir the senses.

Personal Pronouns and Other Personal Reference Words. You should make great use of personal pronouns and other personal reference words. The language of speeches should abound with the pronouns *I, we,* and *you.* We should talk about John, Jim, and Mary. We are concerned about the problems of Frank, Sally, and Tom. Personal pronouns and your personal reference words, along with the names of people, make your speech distinctly more vivid.

Action Verbs. Use action verbs rather than passive or copulative constructions. "Newspaper headlines shout of its nearness; radio announcements cry of its presence; television programs flash this hysteria into our homes." This sentence abounds in action verbs. Contrast "Its presence has been noted by us." Action verbs have the power to excite the senses and make a speech vivid.

Simple Words. Simple words have greater power than multisyllable or affixed words. Affixed words in the main tend to be those that have been derived from the Greek or the Latin and have their meanings modified by syllables added at the beginning or at the end. *Able* is a suffix to the word *comfortable*. *Dis* is a prefix to the word *disavow*. One of the most memorable of all sentences uttered by a speaker, the closing sentence of the great "Cross of Gold" speech by Williams Jennings Bryan is made up of simple Anglo-Saxon words: "You shall not press down upon the brow of labor a crown of thorns; you shall not crucify mankind on a cross of gold." Everyday words are familiar to all members of your audience and do not cause individual members to stop and wonder about the meaning while you go on to the next thought. Simple words will usually do a more effective job for you.

These are but a few of the things to consider in making use of effective words. A word of caution with reference to all stylistic devices. Overuse can be like too much seasoning in food. When the seasoning is so heavy that it calls attention to itself, the flavor of the food is lost. So it is with stylistic devices. When they are overused, they begin to call attention to themselves and thus detract from the thought. In addition, overuse of imagery all the way through will make impossible the building to climax. Thus, your strong action verbs, your greater use of image-bearing words will appear in climactic sections of your speech rather than all the way through. When the ornateness of the style calls attention to itself, it is no longer artistically—or effectively—used.

Utilizing Effective Sentence Structure

The good speaker pays attention to sentence length and structure because certain types of sentences are more effective than others to fulfill the purpose of the speaker.

Simple Sentences Instead of Complex. In the first place, generally speaking, shorter simple sentences are preferred to the complex. The speaker's obligation is to make his meaning instantaneously clear; the long complex sentence often is difficult to follow and should be avoided. Various studies have revealed that the great speakers of the past with simpler styles have tended to use shorter sentences. On the other hand, continuous use of the very short sentence can grow monotonous. Vary your sentence length between short and medium.

Periodic Sentences Instead of Loose. Be alert to the use of periodic sentences rather than loose sentences, particularly when driving toward a climax. A periodic sentence does not give up its meaning until the very end. The loose sentence conveys its meaning almost immediately and would be complete were it to have been ended before it was. In other words, in such sentences the period could have been placed earlier without any particular loss of meaning. Some examples:

> **Loose:** She was an invalid until she was 10.

> **Periodic:** Until she was 10, she was an invalid.

The first sentence is loose because a period could appear after the word invalid; in the second, the period could not be placed earlier. In many cases the periodic sentence is to be preferred, as is true in the foregoing example. If your hearers can be prevented from completing the picture too soon, you will be easier to follow as a speaker. In the example above, the hearer might, in the loose sentence, get a picture of someone who is an invalid and then have to make the readjustment to the age. In the periodic sentence, the clause "until she was 10" will cause hearers to withhold the creation of any image because they know that more is coming. We are not advocating the invariable use of periodic sentences rather than loose ones, but it frequently "economizes the mental effort" of the hearer. Periodic sentences also tend to have power of persuasion superior to the loose, and thus are frequently utilized in building climactic portions of the speech.

Balanced Structure. A speaker should be aware of the rhythmic possibilities of balanced sentence structure. A balanced sentence is one in which words, phrases, or even clauses of one part correspond both in form and in position to words, phrases, or clauses of another part. Here are some examples:

> When reason is against us, we will be against reason.

> The modern generation is more concerned with the achievement of joy than in the joy of achievement.

Parallel Structure. The good speaker will be very aware of the value of parallel structure, which is particularly valuable in the well-worded main headings. Parallel structures are formed when two or more phrases, clauses, or even sentences, have identical or similar grammatical organization. Often this type of structure is used to word an evil of the present system and to show how a new proposal will remove that evil. Note the parallel structure of the two headings: "Further nuclear testing will encourage other nations to develop nuclear weapons . . . A ban on nuclear testing will discourage other nations from developing nuclear weapons." A student was speaking in favor of universal health insurance. The following were the evils in the present system. Note the parallel structure: "Where incomes are lowest, illness is greatest. Where incomes are lowest, medical care is lacking. Where incomes are lowest, medical facilities are lacking."

"Grouping of Three." A special form of parallel structure is the "grouping of three." Often speakers wishing to emphasize some idea and at the same time achieve the rhythmic flow of language will resort to this technique. Three words, three phrases, three clauses, or three sentences will be grouped together for emphasis. Here is an example: "A government of the people, by the people and for the people shall not perish from the earth."

The following examples of groupings of three utilize sentences taken from remarks in praise of Queen Victoria:

> "I would call her Napoleon, but Napoleon made his way to empire over broken oaths and through a sea of blood. This person never broke her word. . . . I would call her Cromwell, but Cromwell was only a soldier and the state he founded went down with him into his grave. I would call her Washington, but the great Virginian held slaves. This person risked an empire rather than permit the slave trade in the humblest villages of the dominion." Making use of a variety of these devices for more effective sentence structure will bring greater persuasion. Beauty of language through sentence structure has the power to stir audiences.

Utilizing Special Rhetorical Devices

To make your speeches more stimulating, more pictorial, more emphatic, consider the use of certain rhetorical devices. Used with restraint and at strategic moments in your speech, they can embellish and enhance your style.

The Direct Question. This is a question asked directly of the members of the audience that you, the speaker, intend to answer for them. It has the power to stimulate people to think and to arouse them from the lethargy of inaction. It serves to build a directness of communication between you and your audience so that it seems more conversational.

The Rhetorical Question. This is a question in which the answer is implied within the question itself. The direct question would be: "What are we going to do about it?" The rhetorical question would be: "Is there any doubt that something should be done about it?" Probably no speech was so filled with direct and rhetorical questions as Patrick Henry's "Give Me Liberty or Give Me Death."

> They tell us, Sir, that we are weak, unable to cope with so formidable an adversary. But when shall we be stronger? Will it be next week, or in the next year? Will it be when we are totally disarmed, and when a British guard shall be stationed in every house? Shall we gather strength by irresolution and inaction? Shall we acquire the means of effectual resistance by lying sublimely on our back and hugging the delusive phantom of hope until our enemies shall have bound us hand and foot?

Dialogue. We are all interested in people and when the ideas of your speech are centered on people, dialogue, revealing how the various individuals feel, helps dramatize your ideas. Allow your voice to reveal such emotions.

Figures of Speech. Figures of speech have power to add beauty and force to your language. They are words or phrases used in a sense other than their literal meaning. Our language abounds in these figures, some of which are so common as to seem literal. There are many different kinds of figures of speech. There is simile: "She can sing like a bird"; metaphor: "She is a lion for courage"; synecdoche, a part standing for the whole: "All hands to the pumps"; metonymy, a word used to represent or suggest another: "The pen is mightier than the sword." All great speakers of the past used figures of speech to a greater or lesser degree, and those utilizing the "grand" style, such as Franklin Delano Roosevelt and John Fitzgerald Kennedy used them in abundance. Embellishing or ornamenting cold logic with figures of speech is often effective. Take care, however, to avoid overuse and trite or overworked figures of speech. Mixed metaphors can confuse and should be avoided.

Literary and Biblical Quotations. Such quotations in the introduction or in the closing part of the conclusion, or even in the body of the speech when you are introducing a new point or when you are trying to climax a point, will add strength. Aptly chosen and used with restraint they have power to move.

The Allusion. An allusion is a brief reference to some experience that all people have in common. To call a woman "a good Samaritan" is an allusion to the story of the Good Samaritan, which is familiar to most people. To say that he is another Romeo is an allusion to Shakespeare's play. One may briefly allude to historical happenings, such as Thomas Jefferson's suggestion that we beware of entangling foreign alliances, or Abraham Lincoln's "We shouldn't change horses in the middle of the stream." We have many common experiences in the various areas of human activity because of similarities in our education and living circumstances. Brief allusions to those common experiences will often touch off springs of response as effectively as telling the complete story. They are particularly effective in enlivening your speech when driving toward the climax.

Comparison and Contrast. The value of comparison and contrast is fairly well known to all. By comparison as a stylistic device we do not mean the reasoning from analogy described earlier, although that is a form of comparison. We intend here the figurative comparisons in which we try to describe the airplane by comparing it to a bird. Usually, whenever we are using a comparison we immediately have to make the contrast, particularly when speaking figuratively. We would have to contrast the motive power of the bird flapping its wings with the gasoline or jet motor of the airplane.

The Long Illustration—Human Interest Story. One of the greatest tools that a speaker can have at her disposal is the long illustration, particularly when it takes the form of a human interest story. Two of these rhetorical devices are similar: the very brief allusion that can be followed by the shorter example that takes only two or three sentences to reveal; the long illustration that may take many sentences to tell and has great power to reveal meaning and to define very accurately what you are trying to suggest with your arguments. It is effective particularly in developing a point after having named it; finally, the long human interest story is one of the most powerful tools of all by which you can arouse the emotions of an audience. The good storyteller has at her command the power to make the audience "become so quiet you could hear a pin drop." The parables and the sermons of Jesus were human interest stories used to make hearers understand. Nineteenth-century American reformer Wendell Phillips's "Toussaint L'Overture" is a speech, the whole of which is a narration of the exploits of that great black leader. The "Acres of Diamonds" speech by famous nineteenth-century orator Russell Conwell contains 17 of these long illustrations; so important were they that his speech could almost be labeled, "Stories of an Idea." The most serious drawback of a long illustration is the time it takes; your time limits may prevent extended use of this device. On the other hand, the long illustration is often more valuable than a quarter hour of statistics.

Repetition and Restatement. These are two of the most important tools of the public speaker. The reader can go back and reread when he forgets or misses the meaning or when his attention wanders. The listener has no such opportunity. Thus the progression of the ideas by the speaker must be slower than those of the writer because of the frequent necessity for repetition or restatement. Repetition is merely saying the same thing over and over. In fact, good main headings should be stated at least three times in the speech and possibly more often.

Restatement is simply the phrasing of the same idea in new or differing words and is particularly effective when citing statistics. If you are trying to suggest that more than 40,000 people were killed in automobile accidents last year, emphasize the importance of this number so your audience gets a better picture of how many 40,000 are. If your school gymnasium seats 5,000, you could suggest that enough people are killed each year to fill that gymnasium eight times.

Keeping the Speech Marching Toward a Goal

Speech, like a journey, should have a destination. The goal is worded in the specific response you desire from the audience. You may not always wish to reveal that specific response to the audience, in which case you substitute another type of goal. Throughout the speech you use certain devices that will keep your speech driving toward that goal. Any speech that lacks this aspect will soon lose the interest of the audience. Several devices can be used to help keep your speech marching. For example, in the introduction, you can partition the speech.

Partition. Partitioning the speech is the process of telling your audience in your introduction the various parts or topics that you plan to elaborate within the discussion. This partition may be quite formal, "I am going to show you, first, that there is a need for a change and, second, that the solution I propose will remove those evils and, third, that it is a workable solution for us." (Such a debater should use better-worded headings!) But it may be more informal, "There have been many questions arising about buying on credit. We've wondered, does it cost too much? We've wondered, what effect does it have on our

economy? Does it make depressions worse? Does it have any effect on inflation?" By outlining ahead of time just what you are going to say, the audience
is more likely to know where you are at any given moment.

Forecast. The forecast is any sentence or a phrase that indicates the subject
you are about to discuss. The partition in the introduction is one special type
of forecast. There are others. Using the words one, two, and three will help
your audience understand where you are in the speech and be able to better
follow your organization. Far too many speakers are fearful of using these
digits; they should discard this fear because these devices aid the audience
in understanding where the speaker is and are helpful in keeping the speech
marching toward the goal. Frequent use is advised, particularly in the argumentative speech.

Summaries. Frequent summaries throughout your speech are essential. In an
argumentative speech, a summary may occur in the conclusion or at other
points. The formal summary is very proper in the speech to influence through
logic, but, should you desire, you may use the informal summary. The summary, of course, is a restatement of what you have already developed.

Conclusion. Another indispensable tool to keep your speech marching toward
a goal is the conclusion. Not only the conclusion at the end of the whole speech
but conclusions you reach throughout. Conclusions are particularly important
in the speech that tries to gain the belief of an audience. Remember, to develop
any point you need to name it, explain it, support it, and conclude it. Note that
with each point you need to draw a conclusion; omitting these conclusions is
one of the most frequent mistakes of novice speakers. To forget to draw the
conclusion that you have been working toward from the beginning is to forget
the goal itself. Remember that the conclusions on the minor points become
the premises on which you build the major points. In concluding and summarizing your minor points, you draw the conclusion on the first, second, and
third issue. Then by restating the premises in the form of conclusions of each
issue, you draw the overall conclusion of your speech.

Suspense and Climax. These two additional elements will help keep your
speech marching toward a goal. While forecasts, summaries, and conclusions
are absolutely indispensable, suspense and climax need not be used but are
extremely helpful. You create suspense when you introduce uncertainty about

how the speech is going to turn out. You may suggest a cause and search for the effect of it or suggest the effect and search for the cause. Again, you can, like the speaker whose topic is buying on credit, raise important questions and create the suspense of wondering what the answer will be. You should alert yourself to the possibilities of suspense and use it to hold the attention of the audience.

To achieve a climactic effect you must build each point so that the response, both intellectual and emotional, is at its greatest peak at the end of the point. As you name the point, the audience at best is only curious, but as you explain it, you satisfy their curiosity. Additional supporting material should arouse the audience emotionally, and your delivery should match this emotional level as it grows within the audience. When you complete the first point, you will relax the audience and then begin the same process for the second point.

By such devices you can keep your speech marching toward your goal and hold the interest of your audience. Like any traveler, your listener will enjoy knowing where she is on this trip through your ideas. Many a speaker is dull because he doesn't know the value of these techniques of forecasting, summarizing, and making conclusions within the speech, or because he ignores such excellent devices as suspense and climax.

ETHOS: PERSUASIVENESS OF THE SPEAKER

Ethos is that element of persuasion that lies within the speaker. It is derived from the speaker's reputation, his position or role in life, the power of his personality, his use of voice, and his use of body.

The Power of Position and Reputation

Some of the persuasiveness of the speaker arises from the position she holds. The manager of a corporation, the chairperson of a college department, or the person who has attained a high position in any area of endeavor carries greater authority and therefore has greater personal persuasiveness. The president of a bank speaks with greater authority than a bank clerk. The persuasive power of any person increases as he grows older and attains higher and higher positions in his chosen profession.

The reputation of a speaker has power to influence others. People who are known to be successful, considerate, honest, and good will derive influence from their reputation. Often prestige in one field will lend greater credence to their speaking in allied fields. Dwight Eisenhower was able to attain great prestige as president because of both his high position in World War II and his reputation for success. Because of both reputation and achievement, he was reelected president of the United States even though Congress became Democratic. Reputation is a valuable asset to any public speaker.

The Power of Personality

Personality is usually defined as persistent tendencies of adjustment, but another definition is more useful for us: Personality is the sum total of others' reactions to us. If a speaker possesses many desirable traits, such as those listed in the discussion on appeals to the sentiments, she will be more persuasive. Certain traits, however, are particularly desirable for a speaker.

Sincerity. Sincerity is one of the more important traits essential to the speaking personality. A speaker must have a genuine concern for the subject that he is discussing, for its importance to the audience present, for its importance to the world. He must radiate his desire to make the audience respond.

Congeniality. Congeniality, or friendliness, is derived from a genuine respect for people. All of us respond strongly to someone who seems to have a genuine interest in us, who is concerned about us, who has affection for all humankind. Any speaker who exudes this "warmth of friendliness" has greater powers to persuade.

Consideration and Kindness. The speaker who understands her fellow humans, is considerate of their feelings, and is kind in her treatment of them will have strong influence on an audience. We all tend to react negatively to the egotistical, self-centered individual. We dislike the braggart. On the other hand, we respond strongly to those who are sympathetic to the problems of others. Humankind honors those who "forget themselves to serve others." In simpler terms, the speaker serves himself best by serving the needs and desires of his audience.

Sense of Humor and Proportion. Having a sense of humor differs from being witty. Many speakers who never attempt to use wit in a speech leave the impression of having an excellent sense of humor. By sense of humor we mean a sense of proportion ". . . all things count but none too much." Many self-appointed reformers lose considerably because they lack this sense of proportion; they arouse strong negative reactions in others and often fail to influence them as greatly as they might. The speaker who is capable of laughing at herself, of smiling at her own slight mistakes, will not only overcome stage fright easily but also have stronger powers of persuasion.

The four traits of personality mentioned here are most important to the speaker. Cultivate them by developing a genuine affection for people and certainly a respect for them and their right to their opinions and their right to disagree. You must learn to "laugh over, laugh with, weep over, and weep with humankind."

The Power of an Effective Voice

Although several good books are available that contain excellent exercises by which any speaker can develop an effective voice, many neglect their voice development. Virtually every human being possesses a musical instrument potentially so beautiful that a violinist merely tries to imitate it. The great organists of the world often attempt to match the unusual beauty of the vocal choir. Yet so many public speakers and others go around with voices that sound like quacking ducks or clucking hens. Many have voices that repel listeners without knowing that they do.

Develop a Basically Pleasing Voice. Your first task in developing an effective voice is to develop a basically pleasing one. The principles involved are simple enough; the drill and practice, however, require fortitude and determination.

First of all, you must always have **plenty of breath support.** Many urge that you discover diaphragmatic breathing. This will certainly do no harm. Others are not quite so certain that this is important. However, all agree that plenty of breath support is needed.

A second essential to a basically pleasing voice is an **open and relaxed throat.** The nasal twang so prevalent in many areas of the country is more often than not the result of a tight throat. Tensions are so common in our fast moving world that many people carry these general tensions over into the throat when they are speaking. The result is a rasping harshness. Unfortunately for most of us, we hear more of our voice through the bones and tissues leading to the inner ear than we do through the air. These bones and tissues act like a tone control, cutting off or reducing the unpleasantness of the sounds we make. The result is that most of us find our own voices more pleasing to ourselves than our voice is to others. Be alert to whether you have a tight throat—almost all of us do when we are excited, as we are when we are speaking in front of audiences. Learn to remove this tension to achieve a basically pleasing voice.

A third essential is to **open the mouth.** Many make too little use of the lower jaw. It not only increases the oral resonance considerably but often has the effect of helping to open up the throat and increase the pharyngeal resonance as well. This improved resonance will not only help develop more pleasing quality to the voice but will also improve enunciation. The tongue, the teeth, and the lips will be used more energetically.

A fourth factor essential to achieving a basically pleasing voice is to energetically use the lips, teeth, tongue, jaw, hard and soft palate, all known as the articulators. It is certainly unpleasant, if not irritating, to auditors when they cannot hear the speaker. Energetic use of the articulators will not only help you get rid of slurring and mumbling, it will also give additional carrying power to your voice. A stage whisper, when the words are enunciated well and when there is plenty of breath for carrying power, can be heard at great distances.

Develop an Interesting Voice. A person filled with the desire to communicate, to get a response from the audience, will seldom have a monotonous voice. Monotony in most cases is the result of lack of motivation on the part of the speaker. In some cases individuals have to drill themselves to develop greater flexibility in the use of voice. You can overcome monotony by drilling yourself to develop your skills in varying the voice and developing greater flexibility.

First, you can work to develop greater variety of **pitch.** Pitch varies as the voice travels up and down the scales (similar to a singer). The only difference between the singing and speaking voice is that the speaker usually travels up or down the scale in rising and falling inflection more rapidly than the singer. Varying the pitch more will often enhance the meaning and reveal finer interpretation. Consider the following sentence: "The teacher says the pupil is a fool." Now consider this sentence: "The teacher, says the pupil, is a fool." Only through sharp contrast in pitch can the human voice make clear in the second sentence that it is the teacher and not the pupil who is the fool. The monotonous voice will always have trouble with the second sentence. In addition, variation of pitch will result from yours emotions about your own ideas or the emotions that you desire to inspire in the listener.

Second, your voice will be more interesting if you vary the **rate**, or speed, of utterance. Your basic rate or average rate should be neither too fast nor too slow. The rate of utterance of the lethargic person is frequently too slow. The rate of the tense person or one who fails to open up her mouth is frequently too fast. Determine what your average rate should be for maximum communication of meaning. Then from this average vary the rate according to the emotional or intellectual content of your speech. Study reveals that rhythm is an important factor in life and that the various emotions have their own peculiar rhythm. Sadness, for example, is slow while anger is rapid. Unusually strong emotion will be quite irregular, now fast and now interrupted. Furthermore, the speaker needs to realize the importance of the pause. The brief pause will indicate the end of a thought, while a longer pause is often used to emphasize or strengthen the response of the audience. It is as though you were giving the audience a moment to let them think over what you have just uttered. Attention to, and drill in, the development of a varied rate is worth your while—it will make your speaking more persuasive.

A third way to make your voice more interesting is to vary its **volume** (intensity). This is probably the best known of all methods for emphasis. The average volume should vary according to the size of the audience. When talking close to an individual your volume need not be very loud; an audience of 25 requires greater volume. An audience of 5,000 takes distinctly more. The average volume of many people is often much too soft, particularly in the classroom where the reciting student is not sensitive to the needs of the people in the far corners of the room. Often untrained or inexperienced speakers will talk to an audience of 1,000 as though only 20 were present. Make sure your average volume is such that the people who are in the back rows can hear you. Once having determined accurately the average volume needed, then for emphasis you can vary your voice from soft to loud. In fact, as you come to the climax of a particular portion of your speech, you will often find your voice getting louder and louder for greater emphasis. Many, however, do not realize that were they to follow that great loudness with tremendous softness (such as a virtual stage whisper), the contrast will bring probably the greatest emphasis, especially if followed by a long pause.

A fourth way to vary the voice to make it more interesting is to vary the **quality**. The quality of the human voice is a function of the amount of tension within the voice and the resonance. At any moment in time, a human is in what could be described as some particular emotional state. Most psychologists suggest that there are basically three emotions: love, hate, and fear. But the public speaker should think of individuals as on a continuum, one in which they fluctuate from intense feelings of love to merely pleasantness to the unpleasant to the extremes of hate and fear. Each of these emotional states then has its own degree of tension that is reflected in the human voice. At any given moment while speaking you will have a certain emotional reaction to your own ideas. These emotional reactions will bring an accompanying change in the quality of your voice, as you desire to emphasize one part of your speech as against another. The quality of your voice should change according to your own emotional reaction or as you desire to suggest an emotion to the listener. Develop the skill of enriching the meaning of what you have to say by varying the quality of your voice. Your own emotional reaction to your ideas and your attitude toward your audience will be the guiding factors. Some speakers find their own emotional reactions an interference. For example, stage fright, in the inexperienced speaker who has not learned to control it, will often be revealed in the voice. We suggest that attention to, and control of, factors that cause quality to vary can be of great help to your powers to persuade. Many students interested in public speaking turn to the reading of poetry for drill; others enroll in courses in oral interpretation to help develop their skills.

Take care when working on developing an interesting voice. Far too many individuals in training their voices have developed a mechanical or artificial sound. Some make you feel like saying, "She likes the sound of her own voice." One should be diligent in avoiding this kind of falsity. "Elocution" fell into disrepute and held back speech training in parts of the world because of these faults. If you have a strong understanding of people and a genuine interest in getting meaning across to them, you will have no trouble. The factors of vocal variation should approximate the kind that take place in animated everyday conversation. In fact, good speaking to audiences can be described as "enlarged conversation."

The Power of Effective Use of the Body

People can reveal much meaning without uttering a word. Complete stories can be told in pantomime. Accompanied only by music, a drama can unfold before our eyes in the ballet. Our manner of walking can reveal that we are in a hurry to get somewhere or that we have lots of time. Without uttering a word many a college student in walking across the campus has said to some member of the opposite sex, "You look pretty good to me." The human body, arms, face, and eyes can reveal meaning to others and, above all, reveal our emotional reactions to our own ideas and to our speaking situation. Furthermore, when we realize that emotion is a total bodily response, we will be alert to the fact that our bodies can detract from our speaking. A slouching body tends to reveal a lackadaisical attitude and little desire for strong emotional response from the audience.

Constant Eye Contact. When speaking to audiences, look specific individuals in the audience directly in the eye. Such eye contact might well be considered the electric current of communication between you and your listeners. Look one person in the eye while you utter an entire sentence or a complete clause. Then move your eyes to the next individual, dwelling long enough to note the reactions on the face of that person. If the audience is small, you may find yourself focusing on one person to your left, a second person in the middle, and a third person to the right. This is all right for practice, but later on you should make a point of looking many members of the audience in the eye. The back wall cannot respond, nor the windows, nor the out of doors, so it is senseless for you to look there. Furthermore, the moment you break from direct audience contact, you are revealing your own lack of desire to communicate. Should you have trouble accomplishing this direct eye contact and this sense of direct communication, a good exercise is to sit in a chair and give the whole speech to a roommate or a member of your family while looking them in the eye constantly. The actor on the stage can seldom, if ever, look the members of the audience in the eyes. The oral reader may from time to time look away, but the public speaker should have strong direct eye contact for greatest persuasion.

Using Facial Expression. The emotion of fear brings a mask to the face; thus the frightened speaker will tend to have less facial expression than usual. In everyday conversation, however, most people's faces are very animated. As public speaking is enlarged conversation, you should make more use of facial expression rather than less. Start your speech with a smile (a token of congeniality) and don't be afraid to frown (this can suggest concern) while now and then you may use a quizzical look. Try to develop an expressive face.

Using Effective Head Gestures. The head can make two gestures: the forward nod for "yes" and shaking from side to side for "no." Infrequently a speaker will shake his head in the "no" gesture. For emphasis, however, make frequent use of the "yes" gesture. Most arm gestures are, or should be, accompanied with the head gesture for emphasis. Many times you will want to emphasize a point but will use only the head gesture without an arm gesture. This may feel a bit strange to you at first, but without head gestures you may appear to be stiff and formal.

Using Effective Arm Gestures. Arm gestures as well as any other total body response or selective response often accompany a strong desire to communicate your ideas to others. When you are responding more strongly to your own ideas, you will have an urgent need for gesturing. In animated conversation you will see some people using a few gestures, others many. Gestures that are planned are usually false and mechanical because they don't arise from an inner urge, but proper gesturing habits can be developed. The public speaker should use complete arm rather than just hand or elbow-to-hand gestures.

Every Gesture Has Three Parts. The first is the approach in which the whole arm swings out and forward from the shoulder. Then comes the meaningful part of the gesture, the stroke, which is descriptive in nature, such as using the two hands to describe the length of a fish; suggestive, in which you indicate that the huge chasm of the Grand Canyon stretched below as you looked from the rim, or emphatic, as though you were going to pound on the table but restrained your impulse. The last part of the gesture is the return. The approach and return should be slow, relaxed, properly timed. The stroke should reveal the meaning you desire. In using one armed gestures, the extended hand should be just below the line of eye contact. In using two armed gestures, eye contact will be between the two extended arms. The maximum amount of movement should be at the shoulder with very little at the elbow. Done properly, the gesture has a nice curved line all the way from the shoulder to the tips of the fingers.

When practicing good gesturing, start with the double armed gesture of appealing to the whole audience, swinging the arms freely at first and then making the gesture. At first all this will seem awkward because when we are sitting our gesturing is chiefly from the elbows. From the platform you should use your complete arm.

Developing Good Posture. The best posture for the public speaker is straight but not stiff. The stance should be similar to that of the boxer, with one foot directed forward toward the audience, and the other one behind and at an angle.

This stance is much better than a military one, which leaves the body stiff and difficult to balance, particularly when you start gesturing. The weight for the most part should be balanced on both feet. When you want to emphasize something or make a gesture, your weight inevitably will swing forward on the ball of the forward foot. On a few occasions your weight may swing back to the heel. From such a position you will always find yourself standing relatively straight and the whole body responding as you gesture.

Move to Enhance the Speech. Once you become an experienced speaker, you will have two occasions when you will want to shift your posture. The first: when you desire to make a transition at the close of the development of one main heading and as you proceed to the next. In fact, a proper semicircular movement to the right or to the left will be as effective as a sentence saying, "I am now through with this point; let us proceed to the next." The second occasion for movement is to provide emphasis. As your speech approaches a climax, you will move gradually toward the audience, so you will be the closest to your audience at your speech's peak. Once the climax is reached, you will move back to your usual position. The inexperienced speaker may encounter a third situation in which movement may be appropriate. If you are suffering from stage fright and your knees are shaking, make some brief movements, including gestures, but be careful not to pace.

Some of you may find making these movements on a platform a little difficult. One of your authors did and was given this effective device for practice. Starting with the boxer's stance as recommended above, move to the left. Move the left foot first, pointing the foot directly toward stage left. Let the body follow that foot, then walk in that direction, then out front, stopping again with the closed-in boxer's stance with either foot in the forward position. Now move back to the right.

You can practice these movements with words to help in your timing. Conclude one part and then start the first words of the next heading at the same moment that the first foot hits the floor. You are now talking on the move. Once you have developed good habits of movement, you will be able to forget about the details, and they will become as habitual as brushing your teeth.

Enthusiastic Desire to Obtain a Response—Avoid Artificialities

You will be effective in delivery only if you have a sincere, genuine, enthusiastic desire to obtain a response from your audience. Far too many speakers develop artificialities in speaking. They gestured because they were supposed to and not because they were genuinely motivated; they developed a beautiful voice for its own sake rather than for greater effectiveness in serving others. They studied variety with no sincere desire to utilize it to enhance the meaning of their speaking for others. Consequently, their technique calls attention to itself and prevents communication. To avoid these pitfalls, you must have genuine interest in people, a sincere concern about getting response from them, and must approach public speaking wholeheartedly.

EXERCISES

1. Define:

    a. Logos

    b. Pathos

    c. Ethos

    d. Style

    e. Primary attention

    f. Secondary attention

    g. Derived primary attention

    h. Basic wants

    i. Blocked wants

    j. Symbols of identification

    k. Emotionally loaded words

    l. Sentiments

    m. An associated attitude

    n. Pitch

    o. Rate

    p. Volume

    q. Quality

    r. Personal reference words

    s. Affixed words

t. Periodic sentence

u. Loose sentence vs balanced sentence structure

v. Parallel structure

w. Direct question

x. Rhetorical question

y. Figures of speech

z. Simile

aa. Metaphor

bb. Metonymy

cc. Synecdoche

dd. Allusion

ee. Repetition

ff. Restatement

gg. Interpreted statistics

hh. Partitioning a speech

ii. Forecast

jj. Transitions

kk. Suspense

ll. Climax

2. What are the relationships among logos, pathos, ethos, and style? Why might it be said that together they have an accumulative effect?

3. What are the steps in persuasion according to:

   a. Brigance?

   b. Monroe?

4. Which of the three seems more applicable to your speaking? Why?

5. List and explain the various factors of attention available to the speaker.

6. What are "appeals to basic wants" and how are they used in speeches?

7. What is the "blocked want hate object" appeal and why is it so effective?

8. What are symbols of identification and how may they be used in speeches?

9. Give examples of emotionally loaded words and tell why they are better to use in a persuasive speech than synonyms that lack such connotations.

10. Explain appeals to sentiments and how they may be used in speeches.

11. What is the "associated-attitude appeal?" Why is it essential in getting a fair hearing from a hostile audience?

12. What are "appeals to prejudice" and how are they used in speeches?

13. The following might be main headings within persuasive speeches. Indicate the type of appeal used and justify your choice:

    a. Trials by judges mean greater justice.

    b. A compact car can save you money.

    c. Osama bin Laden threatens to destroy the infidels.

    d. Government censorship of newsstand literature is a threat to freedom of the press.

    e. To increase the number of Supreme Court justices means packing the Court for political reasons.

    f. If you believe in fair play, then give the Nazis the right to speak.

    g. Ours is the only true church.

14. Bring to class additional examples of main headings that utilize several of the persuasive appeals described in this chapter.

15. Give a series of short speeches each of which predominantly illustrates one of the persuasive appeals.

16. How are emotional appeals used in the conclusion of a speech? In the introduction?

17. When is a subject vivid?

18. What are image-bearing words and why are they more effective? Which of the following words are relatively more image bearing: thought, baseball player, Sammy Sosa, chipmunk, Peter Rabbit, convalescence, et cetera, Model T Ford, Margaret Thatcher?

19. Give examples of:

    a. Personal reference words

    b. Action verbs

    c. Affixed words

20. Read a speech of some great speaker of the past and bring to class examples of:

   a. Periodic sentences

   b. Balanced sentences ·

   c. Parallel structure

   d. "Grouping of three"

21. Read one or more great speeches of the past and bring to class examples of effective use of the following:

   a. Direct question

   b. Rhetorical question

   c. Dialogue

   d. Simile

   e. Metaphor

   f. Synecdoche

   g. Metonymy

   h. Literary quotations

   i. Allusions

   j. Comparison

   k. Contrast

   l. Repetition

   m. Restatement

   n. Partitioning

   o. Forecast

   p. Suspense

   q. Climax

22. Write out a speech in your usual style; then rewrite the speech making extensive use of stylistic devices that will make it more vivid. Be prepared to read the speeches in class or to turn them in to your instructor.

23. Why are reputation and position powerful factors of ethos? Give examples of people who have them.

24. What personality traits enhance the ethos of a speaker? What are some that you would recommend in addition to those mentioned by the author?

25. Why will a basically pleasing voice enhance the ethos of a speaker? What are the four essential elements by which we achieve a basically pleasing voice?

26. Turn to books on voice improvement for exercises to achieve each of four essentials of a basically pleasing voice; be prepared to lead the class in performing at least two of the exercises for each of the four essentials.

27. How does one develop an interesting voice?

28. Turn to books on voice improvement for exercises to achieve improved variation of pitch, rate, volume (force), and quality. Be prepared to demonstrate to the class at least two exercises for each of the four factors.

29. What is the motivation for a speaker to use the body (gestures and the like) while speaking?

30. To what six elements of bodily activity should the beginning speaker pay attention in training to become a better speaker?

31. Describe effective arm gestures.

32. When and how should a speaker move while delivering a speech?

33. What effect does size of an audience have on delivery?